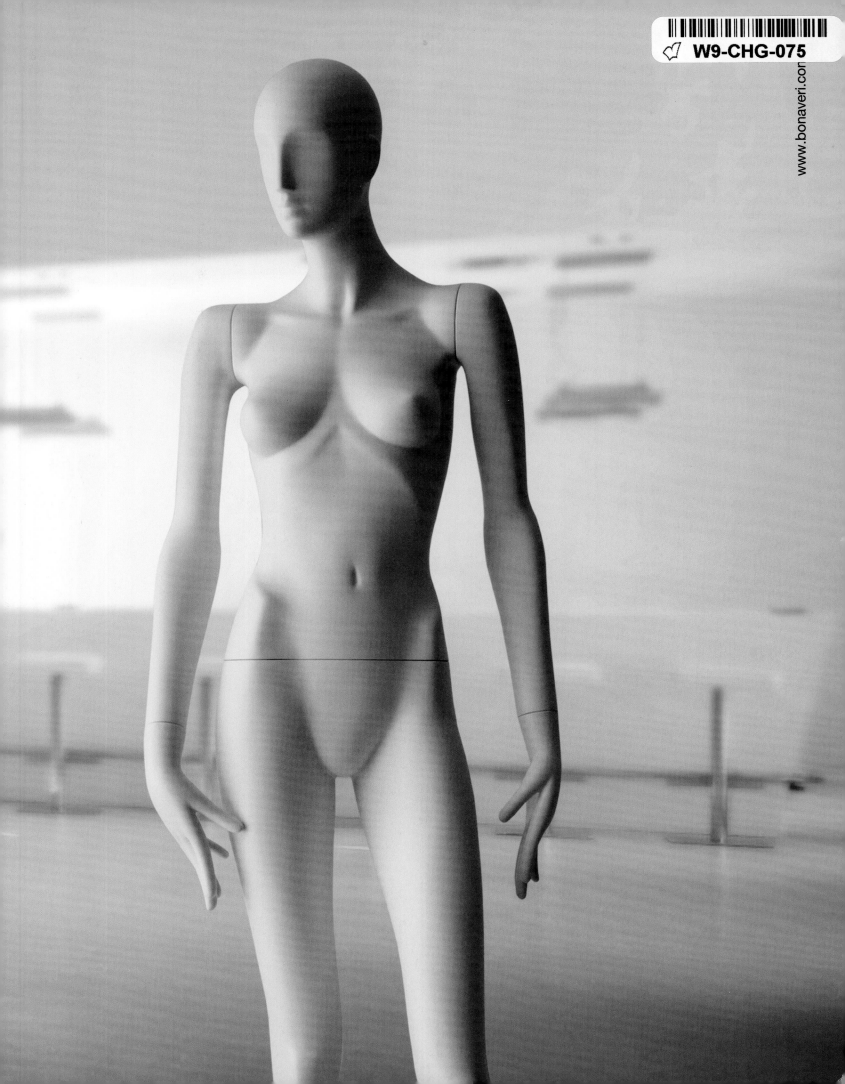

Choose Yourself
Contemporary Portraits by Sicis

GLOBAL EDITION . PATRICK JOUIN

GLOBAL BERNHARDTDESIGN.COM
EUROPE DANERKA.COM

GALAXY FORMING ALONG FILAMENTS, LIKE DROPLETS ALONG THE STRANDS OF A SPIDER'S WEB BY TOMAS SARACENO, PAGE 096

THE GREAT INDOORS : ISSUE 72 : JAN/FEB 2010

FRAM3

STEVEN HOLL : FABIO NOVEMBRE : JAVIER MARISCAL : TOMAS SARACENO : NENDO : ZAHA HADID : JUN IGARASHI : RCJV ARCHITECTS
MICHAEL YOUNG : TOKUJIN YOSHIOKA : PHILIPPE RAHM : THE BOUROULLECS : TADAO ANDO : CLIVE WILKINSON : MINISTRY OF DESIGN

THE SENSUAL WORLD

MUSEUMS — THE NEW WONDER ROOMS
EUROPEAN DESIGN FAIR DISCOVERIES
THE GREAT INDOORS AWARD 2009

CAMPER STORE IN LONDON BY TOKUJIN YOSHIOKA, PAGE 104

THE HERMITAGE IN AMSTERDAM BY HANS VAN HEESWIJK AND MERKX + GIROD, PAGE 126

PUNTA DELLA DOGANA IN VENICE BY TADAO ANDO, PAGE 118

ACTIVE™

CLEAN AIR & ANTIBACTERIAL CERAMIC

The positive effects of **TiO2 dioxide** in the reduction of atmospheric pollution and its antibacterial action are universally known and widely documented, as stated also by Dr. Jennifer Ariss, research scientist for the TCNA (Tile Council of North America).

Fiandre and **Iris Ceramica** have **designed** and **created** a new procedure that maximizes these beneficial effects on ceramic surfaces for both floors and walls (references by the Centro Ceramico of Bologna and the TCNA, **www.active-ceramic.com**, **www.floornature.com**).

FIANDRE®
ARCHITECTURAL SURFACES

iris®
Ceramica

GranitiFiandre spa
via Radici Nord, 112
42014 Castellarano (RE) Italy
www.granitifiandre.com

Iris Ceramica spa
via Ghiarola Nuova, 119
41042 Fiorano Modenese (MO) Italy
www.irisceramica.com

Gregorietti Associati - photo: Lapone/Bolzoni

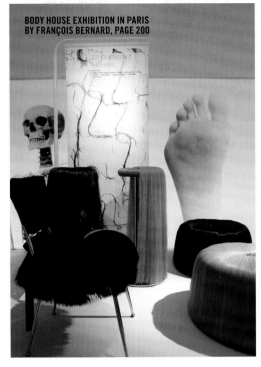

BODY HOUSE EXHIBITION IN PARIS
BY FRANÇOIS BERNARD, PAGE 200

STAND FOR *101 WOONIDEEËN* IN AMSTERDAM
BY INGRID HEIJNE, PAGE 060

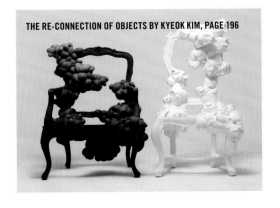

THE RE-CONNECTION OF OBJECTS BY KYEOK KIM, PAGE 196

FRAME
Laan der Hesperiden 68
NL-1076 DX Amsterdam
T +31 20 423 3717
F +31 20 428 0653
info@framemag.com
framemag.com

EDITORIAL
editorial@framemag.com

EDITOR IN CHIEF
Robert Thiemann

MANAGING EDITOR
Merel Kokhuis

EDITORS
Jane Szita, Femke de Wild

EDITORIAL INTERN
Milou Steegman

CONTRIBUTING EDITORS
Shonquis Moreno, Alexandra
Onderwater, Louise
Schouwenberg, Chris Scott
and Michael Webb

COPY EDITOR
Donna de Vries-Hermansader

ART DIRECTION
Roelof Mulder

GRAPHIC DESIGN
Mariëlle van Genderen,
Marco Ugolini and
Johannes Verwoerd

TRANSLATOR
InOtherWords (Donna de Vries-
Hermansader)

**CONTRIBUTORS TO THIS
ISSUE**
Giovanna Dunmall, Lilia
Glanzmann, Kellie Holt,
Cathelijne Nuijsink, Jan-Willem
Poels, Jaclyn Spokojny,
Masaaki Takahashi, Katya
Tylevich, Charlotte Vaudrey

WEB EDITOR
Nils Groot
nils@framemag.com

COVER
Designed by Roelof Mulder

**LITHOGRAPHY AND
PRINTING**
Grafisch Bedrijf Tuijtel,
Hardinxveld-Giessendam

PAPER
300gr Trucard,
135gr Sappi Matt,
115gr Hello Gloss and
100gr IJsselprint

PUBLISHER
Peter Huiberts
peter@framemag.com

DISTRIBUTION
Benjamin Verheijden
benjamin@framemag.com

FINANCE
Sandy Kenswil
sandy@framemag.com

**MARKETING AND
COMMUNICATION**
Fee Pfeiffer
fee@framemag.com

ADVERTISING
Elles Middeljans
elles@framemag.com

Michal Kislev-Reshef
michal@framemag.com

**ADVERTISING
REPRESENTATIVES**
Austria/Germany/Switzerland
Xenia Lange
Wolfram Werbung
Feringastrasse 9a
D-85774 Unterfoehring
+49 89 99 24 93 99 0
+49 89 99 24 93 99 9
wolframwerbung.com
lange@wolframwerbung.com
wolfram@wolframwerbung.
com

Italy
Studio Mitos
Michele Tosato
Via Valdrigo 40
I-31048 San Biagio di Callalta
(TV)
T +39 0422 894 868
F +39 0422 895 634
studio.mitos@tin.it

Spain
Publistar
Vibeke Gilland
Cea Bermúdez 10, Ático
ES-Madrid 28003
T +34 91 553 66 16
F +34 91 554 46 64
vibeke.gilland@publistar-es.
com

United Kingdom
Francine Libessart
T +44 207 704 0944
francine@framemag.com

LICENSE HOLDERS
China
Interior Design China
Brenda Huang
T +86 10 664 226 953 02
brendahuang@idg-rbi.com.cn

Russia
Mediacrat
Alexei Medvedev
T +7 495 627 7841
info@mediacrat.ru

Turkey
Tibet Publishing Group Ltd.
Enis Tibet
T +90 21 229 66 75 8
info@framedergisi.com

SUBSCRIPTIONS
subscriptions@framemag.com
framemag.com

**SUBSCRIPTION
REPRESENTATIVES**
Japan
Memex Inc.
4-9-8 Minamisenba, Chuo-ku
JP-542-0081 Osaka
T +81 6 6281 2828
F +81 6 6258 4440
info@memex.ne.jp
memex.ne.jp

Korea
Le Book/Beatboy
Baegang Building, Kangnam-
gu Shinsa-dong 666-11
KR-135-897 Seoul
T +82 11 746 4862
yourbeatboy@hanmail.net

Singapore
Basheer Graphic Books
Block 231 Bain Street #04-19,
Bras Basah Complex
SG-180231 Singapore
T +65 6336 0810
F +65 6334 1950
bgbooks@singnet.com.sg

SUBSCRIPTION RATES
1-year €95
2-year €180
1-year student €75
2-year student €160

Multiple subscriptions
(to Frame, Mark and/or
Elephant) entitle you to a 15%
discount.
mark-magazine.com
elephantmag.com

HOW TO SUBSCRIBE?
Visit framemag.com or
telephone +31 20 4233 717

FRAME (USPS No: 019-372) is
published bimonthly by FRAME
Publishers and distributed in
the USA by DSW, 75 Aberdeen
Road, Emigsville, PA 17318.
Periodicals postage paid at
Emigsville, PA. POSTMASTER:
send address changes to
FRAME, c/o PO Box 437,
Emigsville, PA 17318-0437.

BOOKSTORE DISTRIBUTORS
Australia
Select Air Distribution Services
T +61 2 9371 8866
F +61 2 93718867
sales@selectair.com.au

Austria
Morawa Pressevertrieb
T +43 1 5156 2190
F +43 1 5156 2881 955
mbaburek@morawa.com

Belgium
IMAPress
T +32 14 42 38 38
F +32 14 42 31 63
info@imapress.be

Canada
LMPI
T +1 514 355 5674
mcoutu@lmpi.com

China
Guangzhou Tang Art Culture
Broadcast
T +86 020 384 834 25
F +86 020 384 823 76
ruby@tangart.net

Denmark
Interpress Danmark
T +45 3327 7744
F +45 3327 7701
rr@interpressdanmark.dk

Dubai
T +971 4 266 5964
F +971 4 265 0939
narain@jashanmal.ae

Finland
Akateeminen Kirjakauppa
T +358 9 121 4330
F +358 9 121 4241
tom.backman@stockmann.fi

France
OFR Systems International
T +33 1 4245 7288
F +33 1 4018 3978
info@ofrpublications.com

Germany
IPS Pressevertrieb
T +49 2225 8801 182
F +49 2225 8801 59182
lstulin@IPS-D.de

Vice Versa Vertrieb
T +49 3061 6092 36
F +49 3061 6092 38
info@vice-versa-vertrieb.de

Greece
Papasotiriou Bookstores
T +30 10 3323 306
F +30 10 3848 254
diamantopoulos@
papasotiriou.gr

Hong Kong
The Grand Commercial Co., Ltd.
T +852 2 570 9639
F +852 2 570 4665
thegrandcc@i-cable.com

Hungary
IPS Pressevertrieb
T +49 2225 8801 182
F +49 2225 8801 59182
lstulin@IPS-D.de

India
SBD Subscription Services
T +91 11 2871 4138
F +91 11 2871 2268
sbds@bol.net.in

Indonesia
Basheer Graphic Books
T +62 21 720 9151
F +62 21 720 9151
info@basheergraphic.com

Israel
World Of Magazines
T +972 9 7487338
  +972 54 6 234333
F +972 9 7484571
wldofmag@netvision.net.il

Italy
Idea Books SRL
T +39 0445 576 574
F +39 0445 577 764
info@ideabooks.it

Japan
Memex
T +81 6 6281 2828
F +81 6 6258 4440
info@memex.ne.jp

Korea
Le Book/Beatboy
T +82 11 746 4862
yourbeatboy@hanmail.net

Middle East
AA Studio
T +961 1 990 199
F +961 1 990 188
aastudio@inco.com.lb

Malaysia
Basheer Graphic Books
T +603 2713 2236
F +603 2143 2236
info@basheergraphic.com

Netherlands
Betapress
T +31 161 457 800
F +31 161 453 161
m.maican@betapress.audax.nl

New Zealand
Magazzino Retail Holdings Ltd
PO Box 9912
Newmarket
NZ-1149 Auckland
info@magazzino.co.nz

Norway
Listo AB
T +46 8 792 46 68
carola.genas@listo.se

Philippines
Fully Booked
T +632 858 7000
jaimedaez@fullybookedonline.
com

Portugal
International News Portugal
T +351 21 898 2010
mario.dias@internews.com.pt

Tema
T +351 21 342 4082
F +351 21 716 6925
belmiro@mail.telepac.pt

Poland
IPS Pressevertrieb
T +49 2225 8801 182
F +49 2225 8801 59182
lstulin@IPS-Pressevertrieb.de

Russia
Mediacrat
T +7 49 5228 4919
arman@mediacrat.ru

Singapore
Basheer Graphic Books
T +65 336 0810
F +65 334 1950
info@basheergraphic.com

South Africa
Magscene
T +27 11 579 2000
F +27 11 579 2080
info@magscene.co.za

Spain
Promotora de Prensa
Internacional SA
T +34 932 451 464
F +34 932 654 883
evelazquez@promopress.es

Sweden
Svenska Interpress AB
T +46 8 5065 0615
F +46 8 5065 0750
susanne.pettersson@
interpress.se

Switzerland
IPS Pressevertrieb
T +49 2225 8801 182
F +49 2225 8801 59182
istulin@IPS-d.de

Taiwan
Long Sea
T +886 2 2706 6838
F +886 2 2706 6109
eric@longsea.com.tw

Turkey
Tibet Publishing Group Ltd.
T +90 21 229 66 75 8
info@framedergisi.com

United Kingdom
Comag
T +44 20 1895 433733
F +44 20 1895 433603
louise.taylor@comag.co.uk

USA
Ubiquity Distributors
T +1 718 875 5491
F +1 718 875 8047
info@ubiquitymags.com

Comag
T +44 20 1895 433733
F +44 20 1895 433603
louise.taylor@comag.co.uk

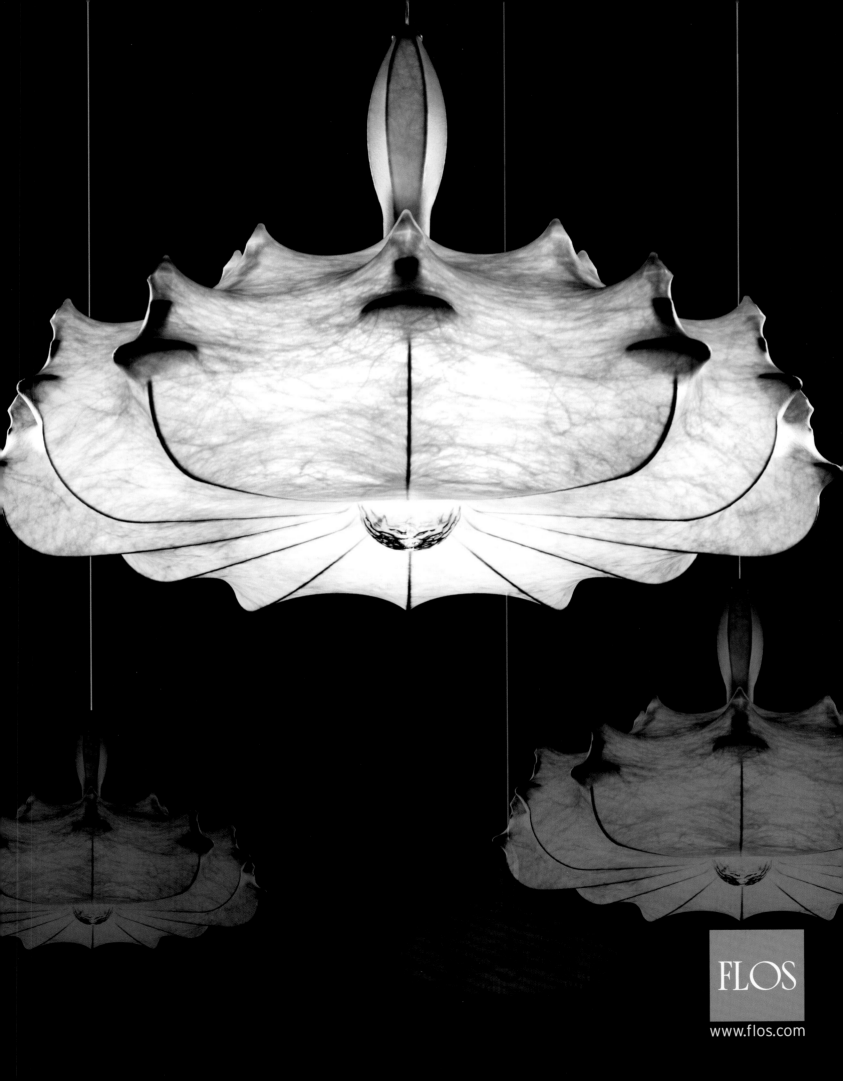

WHEN VANITY BECOMES A VIRTUE

After fifty years in the line of service,
Kevi stands out to add colour to form and function.

Design Jørgen Rasmussen

Engelbrechts

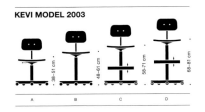

VISIONS

FROM THE DRAWING BOARD

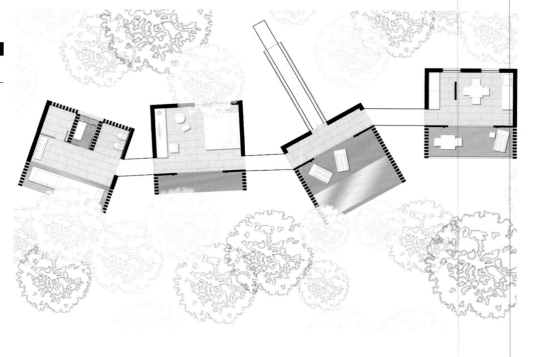

01

NECKLACE, VILLAS IN THE FOREST

■■■ WHO
Ministry of Design
modonline.com

■■■ WHAT
A chain of cubes that forms a series of distinct but seamlessly connected spaces. MOD's hotel design, which can be built in a woodland setting without removing trees from the site, has all the functions of a typical villa: living, dining, sleeping, bathing, swimming and relaxing outdoors.

■■■ WHERE
50 locations in Indonesia

02

DIORAMA HILLS

■ **WHO**
Ja-Ja Architects,
in collaboration with Morten Engel
ja-ja.dk
mortenengel.com

■ **WHAT**
Proposal for a new extension to the Natural
History Museum of Denmark, which is part of a
master plan for Copenhagen's Botanic Garden.
Here zoological, botanical and geological
museums have been united within a single
institute. An interesting and colourful experience
emerges from the combination of atmospheric
rooms and cutting-edge technology.
Competition entry

■ **WHERE**
Copenhagen, Denmark

03

OOGST 1000 WONDERLAND / OOGST 1 SOLO

WHO

Tjep.
tjep.com

WHAT

A self-sustaining project entitled Oogst 1000 Wonderland, consisting of a farm, a restaurant, a hotel and an amusement park. Capacity: 1000 visitors a day. The complex combines fun and functionality. Hotel guests assume the role of farmers. Their work entitles them to free lodgings at the hotel. The design is based on a traditional Dutch farm, but the layout and the technology-controlled agrarian operation are completely new. Oogst 1 Solo is a self-sustaining dwelling that generates food, energy, heat and oxygen for one occupant.

WHERE

Amsterdam, the Netherlands.

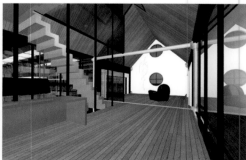

04

UNITED COLORS OF TEHERAN

WHO
Matteo Cainer
matteocainer.com

WHAT
Design for a multistorey office building and a United Colors of Benetton shop. The colourful exterior serves as a means of communication. The philosophy of the Benetton brand is conveyed by Matteo Cainer's coherent and dynamic fusion of exterior and interior design. Competition entry

WHERE
Teheran, Iran

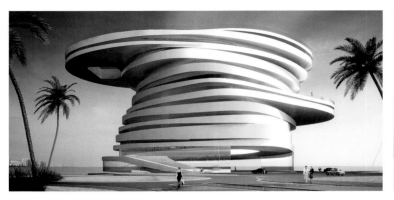

05

HELIX HOTEL

■■■ **WHO**

Leeser Architecture
leeser.com

■■■ **WHAT**

A hotel with staggered floor plates stacked to create an organically shaped volume. Currently under construction, the building has 208 rooms and suites arranged around a helical floor that shifts in width and pitch as it rises to the top level of the building, keeping public spaces constantly in flux.

Winning competition entry

■■■ **WHERE**

Abu Dhabi, United Arab Emirates

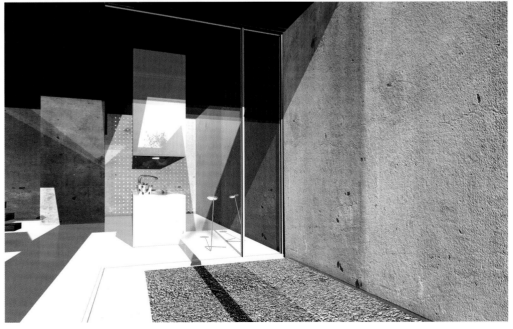

06

2 HOUSES IN TOKYO

WHO
Cheungvogl
cheungvogl.com

WHAT
A pair of nearly identical houses comprising a private residential development known as 2 Houses. House 2a is home to the client; House 2b is for sale. The brief asked for a design that would be calm but not sterile, humble yet unexpected, economical and open, with flexible floor plans. Cheungvogl opted for industrial materials and construction methods and custom-made furniture

WHEN
Expected completion 2011

WHERE
Tokyo, Japan

07

UN/BUILT STORE, CASE STUDY STORE NO. 2

WHO
Assistant, in collaboration with
Item Idem and Mosign
withassistant.net
itemidem.com
mosign.fr

WHAT
A case study for the development of a space-saving retail design requiring virtually no conventional construction techniques. The store is composed of shoe boxes that are simply but methodically assembled according to a specially created plan. As customers buy the products, the store gradually disappears and, at the same time, exhibits the endless variations of the design of Un/Built Store.

WHEN
Expected completion undisclosed

WHERE
Anywhere

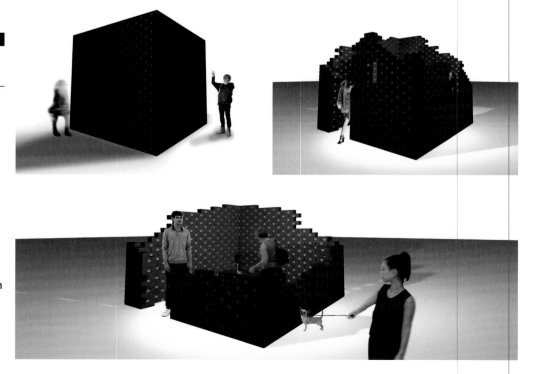

08

BOX 09

■ WHO

Yonoh
yonoh.es
jumpthegap.net

■ WHAT

An independent modular bathroom that offers a range of possibilities geared to the specific needs of the customer. Module 1 holds the water closet, the wash basin, thermal equipment and two water tanks. Module 2 contains the shower, a small seat and two shelves with towel racks. Module 3 can be added if extra space is desired. Competition entry

■ WHERE

Anywhere

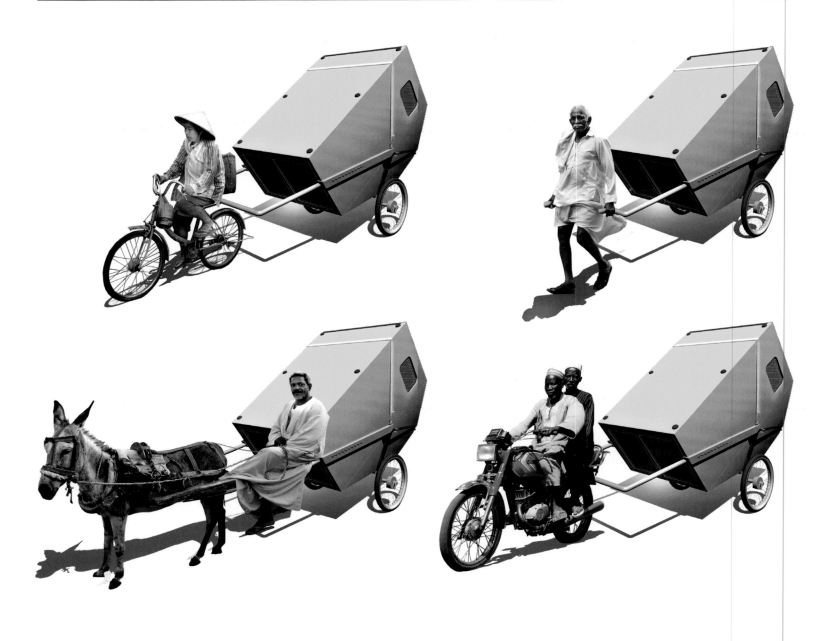

09

ROOM-ROOM

▬▬ WHO
Encore Heureux + G studio
encoreheureux.org
gstudioarchitecture.com

▬▬ WHAT
Proposal for homeless persons worldwide, especially those faced with the problem of moving from place to place. The design addresses climatic, social and political concerns. Room-Room is lightweight, strong, safe, affordable, ergonomic, efficient and easily transportable.

▬▬ WHEN
Expected completion July 2010

▬▬ WHERE
Anywhere

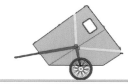

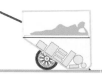

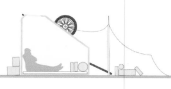

MOVE.

SLEEP.

STAY.

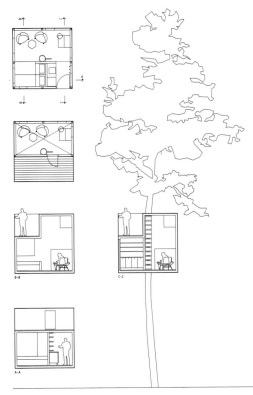

10

HARADS TREE HOTEL

■■ WHO
Tham & Videgård Hansson Arkitekter
tvh.se

■■ WHAT
Hotel accommodation based squarely on the concept of 'back to nature'. Guests are provided with a double bed, a small kitchen, a bath, a living area and a roof terrace. Access is via a rope ladder or a rope bridge attached to a neighbouring tree.

■■ WHEN
Expected completion 2010

■■ WHERE
Harads, Sweden

37ᵗʰ Mostra Convegno Expocomfort

23ʳᵈ-27ᵗʰ March 2010

fieramilano | Exhibition Centre in Rho

MCE™ emotional technology

Mostra Convegno Expocomfort goes straight to the heart of excellence. Technology, innovation, research and design: Mostra Convegno Expocomfort, the world's leading exhibition in HVAC, plumbing and sanitary fitting sectors, scheduled for 23ʳᵈ-27ᵗʰ March 2010, is back. The global showcase offering products, solutions, events, conferences, thematic itineraries and targeted focus that no-one can afford to miss.

Heating | Implements and tools | HVAC components | Air-conditioning, ventilation | Refrigeration | Insulation | Plumbing technology | Water treatment | Renewable energies | Home and Building automation | Taps and fittings | Ceramic sanitary ware | Bathroom accessories

www.mcexpocomfort.it

EXPOBAGNO™

NEXT ENERGY™

organised by

Reed Exhibitions®

A glance in the creative world, because "design is to share"
DESIGN /// ARCHITECTURE /// FASHION /// ART

www.yatzer.com

www.sonyericsson.com/pureness

XPERIA™

Sony Ericsson

make.believe

'We will need to adapt quickly to rapidly altering global conditions – climatic, economic, social and technical'
PIA EDNIE-BROWN

STILLS

PORTFOLIO OF PLACES

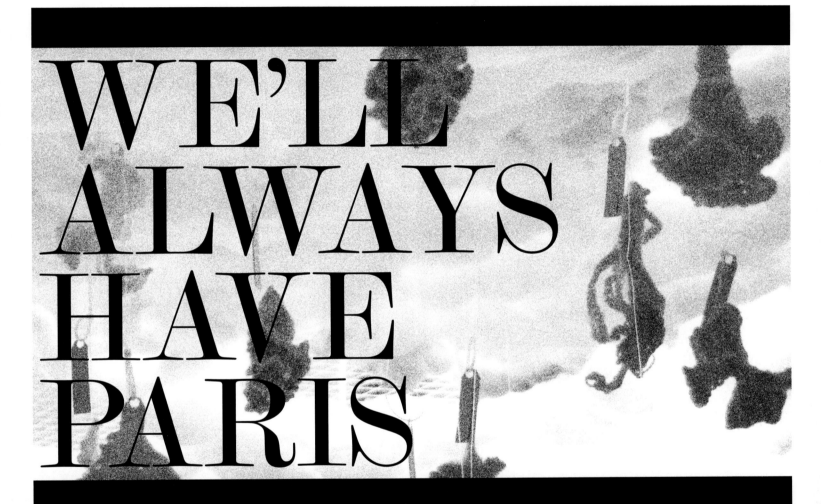

WE'LL ALWAYS HAVE PARIS

How do contemporary designers deal with the iconic status of Paris, the world's most visited city? PASCAL GRASSO's Parisian rooftop restaurant, which shares the skyline with the Eiffel Tower, features a metallic skin whose rows of LEDs provide a shifting aurora borealis of light effects. Prada's pop-up store appropriates the City of Light by mimicking the Pont Mirabeau, while PHILIPPE RAHM fills the archetypally Parisian Grand Palais with an abstract, light-reflecting landscape called White Geology. Meanwhile, R&SIE(N)'s I'mlostinParis, which houses a family of four, challenges expectations of civilized style by disappearing behind a wall of ferns.

Asobio Channel One

BY NENDO

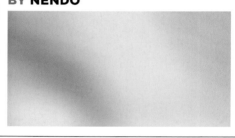

ASOBIO'S FIRST SHOPPING-MALL UNIT IN SHANGHAI IS A SPACIOUS, BI-LEVEL, BLACK-AND-WHITE INTERIOR BY NENDO.

In mid-2009 a new shopping centre opened in Shanghai. The complex, Channel One, recently welcomed Asobio, an Italian fashion label whose latest outlet is the work of Japanese designer Oki Sato of Nendo. 'The shop's theme is "focus",' says Sato, 'so we put monotone photographs of leaves on walls and floor, varying both the sizes – to imitate the effect of a camera's zoom lens – and the sharpness, as a reference to images that are out of focus.' His design solution gives the space depth and continuity, provides diversity, and makes the products on display appear to be 'in focus' in contrast to the decorative patterns. Another contrast is formed by a coal-black staircase and several black walls, which stand out distinctly against their nearly pure-white – and oh, so sweet – surroundings. Sato used wall displays for half the collection and spread the other half on tables in the centre of the shop.

nendo.jp

WORDS **MEREL KOKHUIS**
PHOTOS **JIMMY COHRSSEN**

THE GRISAILLE ON THE GROUND-FLOOR FAÇADE OF THE TEMPORARY SHOP REFERS TO THE FIRST METAL BRIDGE BUILT IN PARIS.

Prada Paris Place Beauvau

BY ROBERTO BACIOCCHI

Like the weather, an economic depression invariably gives way to clear skies. Here and there creative fantasies emerge that might never have seen the light of day had unrestrained consumer frenzy continued. In ten years, will we look back longingly on today's remarkable ephemera, fleeting retail wonderlands and limited collections? Who can tell? What we do know is how much fun it is to step into a five-months-and-it's-gone Prada paradise on the Place Beauvau in Paris and snap up a gorgeous grey-leather bag. Architect Roberto Baciocchi, who showcased the City of Lights in his design for the former gallery, crafted a façade that refers to the first metal bridge in Paris: the Mirabeau. Inside the dual-level space, stylish mannequins appear to be strolling along Parisian avenues or discussing the latest fashions. Shoppers find colourful *tableaux vivants* of *bohémiennes* against backdrops of lilac (downstairs) and beige (upstairs) furniture, complemented by displays of bronzed metal and glass. An altogether charming interior. Oh lá lá, Paris!

baciocchi.it

WORDS **ALEXANDRA ONDERWATER**
PHOTOS **MARIO CIAMPI**

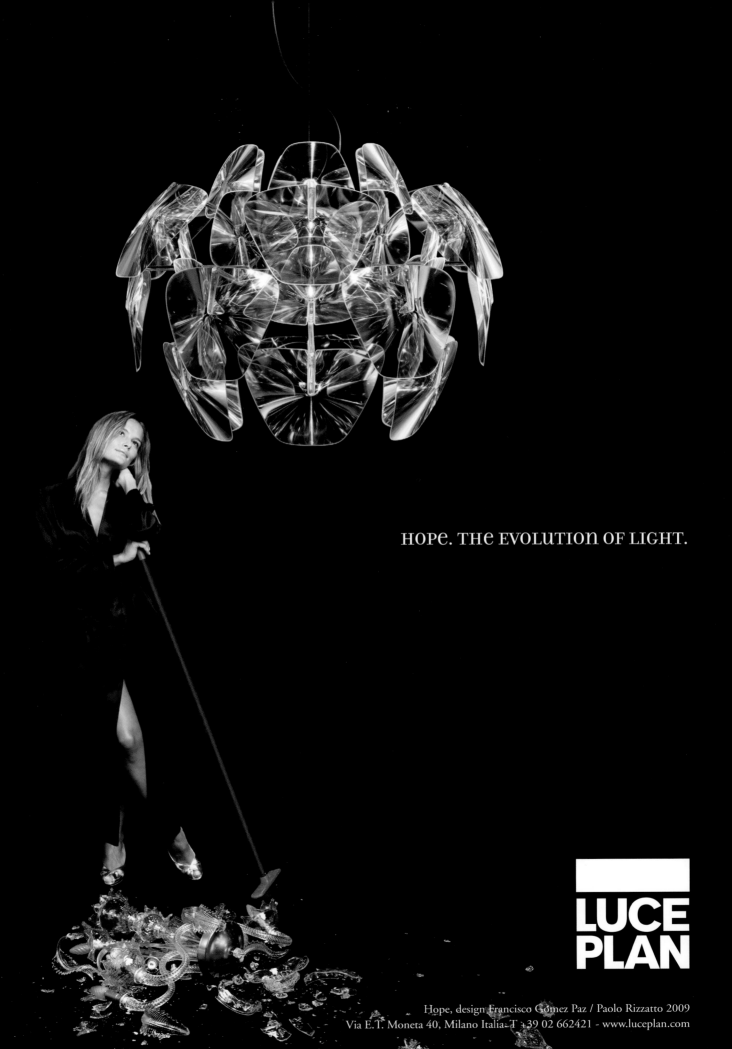

HOPe. THE EVOLUTION OF LIGHT.

LUCE
PLAN

10 ans! 2000 > 2010
HAPPY BIRTHDAY
now!
design à vivre

January 22-26, 2010. international home design exhibition
Paris Nord Villepinte, hall 7. www.nowdesignavivre.com

Trade only. SAFI organisation, a subsidiary of Ateliers d'Art de France and Reed Expositions France
SAFI - 4, passage Roux. 75850 Paris Cedex 17. France
Tel. + 33 (0)8 11 09 20 09. Fax. + 33 (0)1 30 71 46 95. maison-objet@expandsolutions.fr
Visitors: Promosalons. Tolstraat 127. 1074 VJ Amsterdam
+31 / (0)20 462 00 20. +31 / (0)20 463 87 02. maison&objet@promosalons.nl

now!
design à vivre

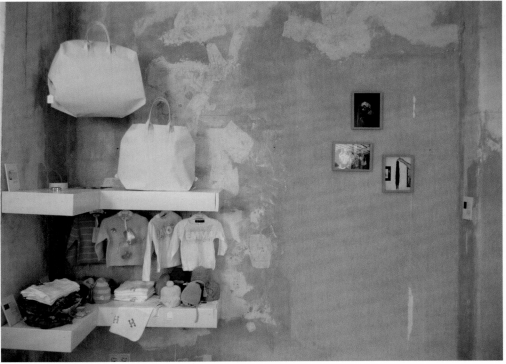

THE SUPERRANDOM SHOP, LOCATED IN MUNICH'S THRIVING HAIDHAUSEN DISTRICT, IS GRAVITY'S CREATIVE NETWORK IN THE FORM OF A RETAIL SPACE.

Superrandom

BY GRAVITY

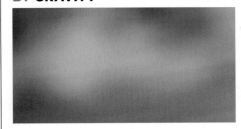

A quirky little shop recently opened for business in Munich's bustling Haidhausen district. Although the name Superrandom suggests otherwise, the store sells 'clothes, design and things of value' that have undergone a strict selection process. 'We focused on quality, not quantity,' says Alexander Grots of Gravity. 'The store interprets authenticity as the clear communication of a product's origins and making-of story. Superrandom spotlights the designers behind the products. You can discover local labels here, as well as work by young unknowns. Our own creations are also on display.' The interior design speaks of somewhat less precision. Pendant lamps by Erco are possibly the only permanent part of the space with an 'ordinary' price tag. Ignoring walls marred by peeling paint, Gravity used wood, tile and other DIY products to make displays, a collage of materials that the designers installed and painted chartreuse to form a uniform entity.

gravity-europe.com

WORDS **MEREL KOKHUIS**
PHOTOS **COURTESY OF GRAVITY**

Double 00'09

BY CASE-REAL

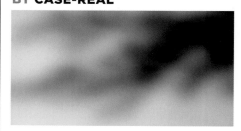

Located on the ground floor of a commercial building in Tenjin – the central district of Fukuoka, 'trend capital' of Kyushu – eager shoppers find the recently opened Double 00'09. The curving wall of this impressive boutique draws pedestrians inside, where they find themselves under a vaulted ceiling in a rather cave-like space that resembles a minimalist house. Designer Koichi Futatsumata, who heads Case-Real, says: 'I thought expressing the richness of the space was important, whereas impressing people with materials and colour was unnecessary. Consequently, I emphasized the lines and planes of the interior.' The result of his decision is a retail environment in which the items on display are shrouded in an aura of simplicity. Futatsumata translates his design philosophy, with its focus on spiritual depth, into spaces made to be cherished for a long time, even those intended strictly for commercial use.

casereal.com

WORDS **MASAAKI TAKAHASHI**
PHOTOS **HIROSHI MIZUSAKI (LOOP)**

GENTLE CURVES CREATE A HARMONIOUS INTERIOR WITH A DISTINCTLY SPIRITUAL AURA.

Change your door...

DOOR
ACCESSORIES

☐ DECORATIVE
FURNITURE
FITTINGS

Tel: (+90216) **561 11 40** Fax: (+90216) **311 36 03**   www.cebidesign.com

INDUSTRIAL PIPING REFERS TO AN ERA
IN WHICH JEANS WERE WORN EXCLUSIVELY
AS WORK CLOTHES

Nature Factory

BY SUPPOSE

A maze of industrial PVC piping 'grows' like branches in all directions at the 65-m^2 Diesel Denim Gallery in Aoyama. The installation, entitled Nature Factory, was conceived by designer Makoto Tanijiri of Suppose Design Office. Pipes hug the wall like vines, cover the ceiling like leaves, stand erect in groups like tree trunks - and have a total length of a kilometre. The shadows they cast on white display elements are like those found beneath the spreading limbs of a tree on a sunny day, although some of the shadows are simply paintings made by Shuhei Nakamura.
The theme is the union of the organic and the inorganic, as represented by the suggestion of a tree and the industrial tubing, respectively. Tanijiri, who established his office nine years ago, has completed more than 60 intriguing housing projects. His creative energy crosses the lines between genres and countries, continuing to surprise his audience.

suppose.jp

WORDS **MASAAKI TAKAHASHI**
PHOTOS **TOSHIYUKI YANO (NACÁSA & PARTNERS)**

cebi ®

☐ **DECORATIVE FURNITURE FITTINGS**

Old passion

new fashion

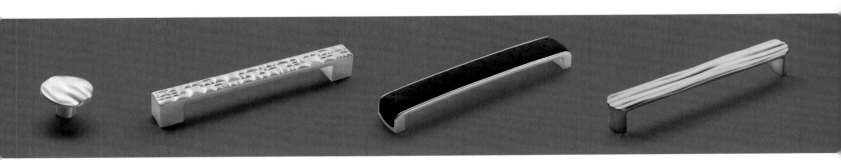

GYPFRAME SHELVING, YELLOW INDUSTRIAL PVC CURTAINS, CONSTRUCTION-SITE LIGHTING, METAL-GRID LOCKERS, SHRINK-WRAP AND STENCILLED SIGNAGE ALL BELONG TO THE WAREHOUSE VERNACULAR.

Dr. Martens Pop-Up Store

BY CAMPAIGN

The interior of the first Dr. Martens pop-up store resembles that of a warehouse, a building type that's been used for temporary retail spaces before (see, for example, 'Louis Vuitton/ Underground' in *Frame* 71, page 33). In this case, however, it refers to Doc Martens' brand identity, says Philip Handford, creative director of design firm Campaign.

Tell us about the brief you got from Dr. Martens.
The design had to express part of the Covent Garden store vernacular, be replicable in any location worldwide, be easy to assemble and source, be unique to Dr. Martens and be very low-cost.
Why did you choose a warehouse look?
The warehouse look and feel were inspired by Dr. Martens' heritage, which Martin Roach described perfectly when he wrote that the boot 'catapulted from a working-class essential to a countercultural icon. . . .
The postmen, factory workers and transport unions who had initially bought the boot by the thousand, were joined by rejects, outcasts and rebels from the fringes of society.'
How much time did you have?
The design process took approximately three months from conception to completion. Construction was realized in six days.

campaigndesign.co.uk

WORDS **FEMKE DE WILD**
PHOTOS **HUFTON+CROW**

We are taking joy seriously...

GOURD-LIKE GLASS APPENDAGES HOUSE A BACTERIA FARM,
WHILE FERNS COVER THE ENTIRE EXTERIOR
OF THIS ECCENTRIC HOME.

I'mlostinParis

BY R&SIE(N)

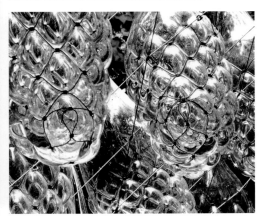

Eco architecture doesn't come any darker or stranger than R&Sie(n)'s Parisian hideaway, an eccentric home for a family of four that's appropriately called I'mlostinParis. Tucked away in a courtyard beneath a forest of ferns, the façade of the house is hung with the gourd-like glass appendages of – wait for it – a bacteria farm. While the 1200 ferns cloaking the three-storey building are fed by hydroponic tubes transporting water from the rooftop, the 300 specially made glass bulbs contain rhizobia bacteria and water. This bacterial soup brews in the summer sunlight and is harvested later as food for the ferns. 'The client had a desire for stealth,' says architect François Roche, explaining the greenery-swathed building. He describes the house as incorporating 'nature gone wild', thanks to its distinctly unnerving bacterial processes – an antidote, certainly, to the pervasive (and, dare we say it, bland) wholesomeness of all too many green architecture projects.

new-territories.com

WORDS **JANE SZITA**
PHOTOS **COURTESY OF R&SIE(N)**

THE DOUBLE FAÇADE OF THE HOUSE IN JIGOZEN IS BOTH
AN AESTHETIC ELEMENT AND A MEANS OF PROTECTION.

House in Jigozen

BY SUPPOSE

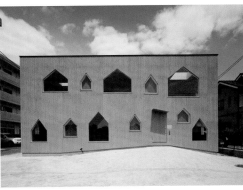

Living in Hiroshima, on the coast of the Inland
Sea, is often a combination of fun and fear,
thanks to the threat of typhoons. Suppose
Design Office's Makoto Tanijiri's house in Jigozen
substitutes enjoyment for the anxiety related to
damage and flooding. Living areas at the core
of the house are embraced by a large communal
envelope, giving the occupants, a young couple
and their child, a buffer zone that cushions the
boundary between indoors and outdoors.
The buffer – for use as sun lounge, veranda,
terrace or garden – forms a safe yet dynamic

shell that both unites and separates interior and
exterior. Tanijiri's construction method is equally
safe and simple. A skeleton featuring diagonally
positioned columns provides both the necessary
support and diagonal stability. Cleverly designed
windows offer great views of the sea.
'If you follow the diagonal lines,' he says, 'what
you get are windows in the form of a house
with a pitched roof.'

suppose.jp

WORDS **CATHELIJNE NUIJSINK**
PHOTOS **COURTESY OF SUPPOSE DESIGN**

AFTER LISTENING TO THE CLIENT DESCRIBE ESSENTIAL 'SCENES OF DAILY LIFE', THE ARCHITECTS TRANSLATED HIS WISHES INTO A RESIDENTIAL INTERIOR.

DG-House

BY GENETO

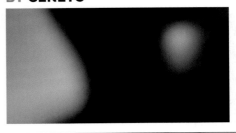

This private residence was designed by Geneto, a group of architects that includes the Yamanaka brothers, among others. They have a workshop in Kyoto devoted to making wooden furniture. This facility enables them to fuse architecture with furniture, an approach that characterizes their design strategy. 'We had been exploring the possibility of making a space richer with something that would be less significant than architecture but more significant than furniture,' says Yuji Yamanaka. The ensuing project includes very few pieces of furniture. Instead, they created objects from 24-mm-thick structural plywood and combined them in different configurations to satisfy the client's various living requirements. Harmonizing with the interior, the flexible objects replace conventional furniture and storage. They have been painted black, but the wood grain is visible upon close inspection. From a distance, these solid black volumes follow the lines of the white walls to create a serene atmosphere.

geneto.net

WORDS **MASAAKI TAKAHASHI**
PHOTOS **TAKUMI OTA**

Beam seat

by Alain Berteau

LENSVELT

Minervum 7003 ▪ NL-4817 ZL Breda ▪ T +31 76 57 22 000 ▪ F +31 76 57 22 022 ▪ E info@lensvelt.nl ▪ www.lensvelt.nl

THIS 86-M² STEEL-CLAD SPACE IS NOT A RUSSIAN MOVIE SET
BUT ARCHITECT PETER KOSTELOV'S PRIVATE RESIDENCE.

Moscow Metal Apartment

BY **PETER KOSTELOV**

The home that Peter Kostelov realized for his personal use is based on the Russian architect's 'desire to create an indivisible architectural design'. For reasons of practicality, he omitted any sort of decoration, choosing instead to focus on functionality and a design that would 'unify all elements of the space'. Located in Moscow, Kostelov's apartment features walls clad in metal, part of a material palette that also includes natural cobblestone, brown cork tile and purpose-designed textile. Although most contemporary architects and interior designers have a tendency to remove the walls of an interior to create one spacious, open-plan area, Kostelov opted for a dwelling with many rooms: living room, bedroom, study, library, two closets, kitchen, bathroom and, for guests, a lavatory and shower. He lowered the ceiling to allow for the insertion of an entresol, which he uses for storage.

kostelov.ru

WORDS **MEREL KOKHUIS**
PHOTOS **ZINON RAZUTDINOV**

House H

BY **SOU FUJIMOTO**

Large transparent surfaces within the already limited floor area of a city residence? A reduction of the occupants' living space does seem rather inefficient, but it was the deliberate choice of architect Sou Fujimoto. It's true that his decision left less room for furniture, but compensation lies in the incredibly spacious atmosphere experienced in the small rooms of this house. Another space-maker is Fujimoto's design of half-open rooms. 'The clients didn't have a need for separate bedrooms with lots of privacy,' he says. 'The construction itself is rather simple: a box-shaped building containing four equally sized rooms. Stepped floors and heights, however, result in a space with both rooms and not-rooms.' Fujimoto added stairs that lead nowhere: 'We installed two fake flights of stairs, which enhance the sense of spaciousness and extend farther than the exterior walls. They even seem to be going in the wrong direction.'

sou-fujimoto.com

WORDS **MEREL KOKHUIS**
PHOTOS **IWAN BAAN**

TWO FAKE FLIGHTS OF STAIRS ENHANCE THE SENSE OF SPACIOUSNESS IN THE 125-M² CONCRETE BOX.

27 t/m 29 januari 2010 Ahoy, Rotterdam

MATERIAL XPERIENCE

Hét materiaalevenement voor architecten, interieurarchitecten en andere creatieve professionals. Het event vindt gelijktijdig plaats met de beurzen Gevel en Licht & Architectuur.

Voor een gratis toegangskaart en het programma gaat u naar:

WWW.MATERIALXPERIENCE.NL

Material Xperience wordt georganiseerd door:

HELENA GULLSTRÖM CREATED LOFTY PROJECT, A SPACE IN WHICH SHE LIVES AND WORKS AS BOTH HAIRDRESSER AND ARTIST.

Lofty Project

BY **HELENA GULLSTRÖM**

'I've always wanted the kind of salon where people could come and have a glass of wine,' says Helena Gullström, discussing the space that currently accommodates her hair salon, artist's studio and private residence. Since moving in a year ago, Gullström has knocked down three walls of her Los Angeles loft and added one: a swivel wall secured by plumbing fixtures. The wall, like most elements between the tall ceilings and concrete floor, is a DIY endeavour. 'I love building,' says the painter-cum-sculptor-cum-hairdresser. The swivel wall, envisioned as a canvas for visitors' art and graffiti, presently veils storage space and Gullström's bedroom. Central to the loft's eclectic design is the constant presence of faces and figures; mingling amidst photos, sculptures and a mannequin are clients, a co-worker, friends and neighbours. 'It's like *Melrose Place*,' she laughs. Then, knocking on the wood of a table she sanded herself, she adds 'without the drama'.

helenagullstrom.com

WORDS **KATYA TYLEVICH**
PHOTOS **KALIM**

CREATIVITY ALSO NEEDS A PLAYING FIELD

Design Indaba bookings are now open. See the best of the best battle it out in an international arena as South Africa's local talent, the Superstars, take on the international All Stars at the premium creative event of the year. The 13th Design Indaba Conference 24 – 26 February and Expo 26 – 28 February 2010. Cape Town, South Africa. **www.designindaba.com**

DESIGN INDABA
A BETTER WORLD THROUGH CREATIVITY

BROUGHT TO YOU BY:

WOOLWORTHS
the difference

ABSA

Grolsch

DStv
so much more

PRODUCED BY:

interactive africa

DEVELOPMENTAL PARTNER:

THIS CITY WORKS FOR YOU

SUPPLIERS: THE JUPITER DRAWING ROOM, SAPPI, BIZCOMMUNITY, CHAYWA, SOUTH AFRICAN TOURISM, KULULA

THE PSYCHEDELIC SEQUENCES OF CELL INTERNATIONAL'S LIGHTING KALEIDOSCOPE WERE GENERATED THROUGH USER INTERACTION.

Lighting Kaleidoscope

BY CELL INTERNATIONAL

As if to prove its credentials as 2010's World Design Capital, Seoul's recent edition of its annual Living Design Fair showcased an array of inspirational installations by Korea's foremost design names, such as Bae Dae Yong, Choi Si Yuong, Jeon Shi Hyoung and Youngse Kim. While many of these favoured the kind of traditional and contemplative simplicity usually referred to as 'Zen-like', a more technological approach was taken by Cell International's design team for its Lighting Kaleidoscope, a 'media effect box' made using the company's LED Boky3 panels. Composed of square pixels that create abstract moving images and generate a range of no fewer than 16,700,000 colours (although we're not sure how they counted them), the panels interact with people, changing hue and shape in response to variations in sound and movement. The result? Pure psychedelic geewhizzery that visitors found compulsive.

zcell.kr

WORDS **JANE SZITA**
PHOTOS **SERGIO PIRRONE**

WITH FABRIC, WOOD, PAINT AND WATERPROOF FELT-TIP PENS, INGRID HEIJNE MADE A STAND UNRIVALLED AT THE AMSTERDAM HOME FUNRITURE FAIR.

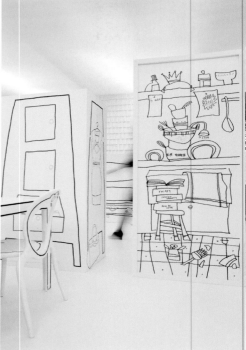

Stand for *101 woonideeën* magazine

BY INGRID HEIJNE

Brief

Design a stand for Dutch magazine *101 woonideeën* (101 ideas for the home) based on the following guidelines:
- Unique, surprising, amusing
- Bizarre yet recognizable
- Open character

Concept

Paging through a magazine lifts you from your everyday existence to give you a moment detached from reality. At this trade-fair stand, you literally step into the pages of the magazine to enjoy a total experience in three dimensions.

Design

By folding two-dimensional sheets of paper, Ingrid Heijne created a three-dimensional world. Her stand design is an exciting play of shapes, surfaces and textures that together form an artistic composition.

Implementation

Heijne's hand-drawn lines have different thicknesses. There's a coarseness in this linearity that is both graphic and abstract. Lines and drawings on walls, partitions and floor – as well as on furniture and products – instantly stir the imagination. What's real and what isn't?

ingridheijne-interiordesign.com

WORDS **MEREL KOKHUIS**
PHOTOS **HUGO THOMASSEN**

Rib for Life

The all new stackable eco chair "RIB" from Johanson Design
Design by Alexander Lervik

RIB – TWO TIME AWARD WINNING CHAIR
BEST OF THE BEST Award by 100% DESIGN in Rotterdam 2009
THE MOST INNOVATIVE NEW PRODUCT Award by Forum AID + 1
at the Stockholm Furniture Fair 2009

Johanson Design Benelux & France   Haarlem (NL) – Tel +31-(0)235514707 | Johanson Design U.K. & Ireland   WARWICKSHIRE (U.K.) | Johanson Design other countries   Markaryd (SE) – Tel +46-(0)43372500
Arthur Eltink Agencies   info@arthur-eltink-agencies.nl | Boline International   Tel +44-(0)1608662010 | Johanson Design AB   info@johansondesign.se
                                                                           | info@boline.co.uk | www.johansondesign.se

SUGAWARA'S VERSATILE OFFICE SPACE WAS INSPIRED
BY THE TOPOGRAPHY OF JAPANESE LANDSCAPE DRAWINGS.

Flow

BY DAISUKE SUGAWARA

In order to incorporate five functions – working, meeting, waiting, reception and display – into the small office space of a Tokyo paper company, designer Daisuke Sugawara drew inspiration from the topography of Japanese landscape drawings. 'This project integrates cutting-edge 3D computer technology with traditional Japanese architectural space,' he explains. 'To heighten the perception of the space, I aimed for the look of a landscape with a topographic form.' Complex, sweeping, wooden shelving units work variously as partitions, display areas, counters, benches and screens, each function flowing seamlessly into the others. 'This design enables not only multiple functions and areas, but also diverse experiences,' comments the

designer. 'These experiences are created by shifting forms of space, the texture of the wooden object, and the changing light and shadow as we walk through it. The interior seems both modern and human, artificial and natural, and simple and complex in terms of atmosphere – reminding us of time spent in fields or mountains.'

sugawaradaisuke.com

WORDS **JANE SZITA**
PHOTOS **KOICHI TORIMURA**

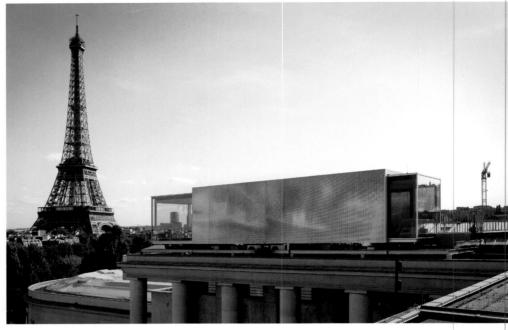

A 63-M² RESTAURANT DESIGNED BY PASCAL GRASSO
TEMPORARILY OCCUPIES THE ROOF OF LE PALAIS DE TOKYO IN PARIS.

Nomiya

BY **PASCAL GRASSO**

If you haven't yet managed to reserve a table at the Patrick Jouin-designed Jules Verne Restaurant in the Eiffel Tower, don't despair. For the time being, you can enjoy a magnificent view of the Eiffel Tower from Nomiya, a temporary 'private' restaurant on the roof of Le Palais de Tokyo in Paris. As a follow-up to Hotel Everland, designed by Sabina Lang and Daniel Baumann in 2008, a new volume presently perches atop the Parisian museum. Architect Pascal Grasso's easy-to-dismantle, transportable structure has a perforated sheet-metal frame and a glazed façade. Interior walls and furnishings are made from Corian. The dimensions of the 12-seat dining venue are 18 x 4 x 3.50 m (l x w x h); the entire unit weighs 22 tonnes. Lighting installed between the restaurant's glass and metallic skins features rows of colour-changing LEDs, which can be programmed to produce breathtaking images that resemble the aurora borealis.

pascalgrasso.com

WORDS **MEREL KOKHUIS**
PHOTOS **NICOLAS DORVAL-BORY**

CALL FOR ENTRIES

Get your designs published in the definitive book on trade fair stands.

Have you recently designed an extraordinary trade fair stand? Then your project and company profile could be included in Frame Publishers' upcoming book *Grand Stand 3: Design for Trade Fair Stands.*

▸ *Grand Stand 3* will contain approximately 180 cases totalling 520 pages of remarkable trade fair presentations from all over the world.
▸ If you want to publish your work in *Grand Stand 3*, contact us for the terms and conditions at books@framemag.com.
▸ Deadline for entrance 1 February 2010. *Grand Stand 3* will be for sale in fall 2010.

↑
YOUR PROJECT IN HERE

Project name

Your name

Project description

Profile of your company

Project credits

Your company address will be included in an index in the back of the book.

FRAMEMAG.COM

THE BLACK SPACE WRAPPED ROUND WITH WHITE RIBBON
REFLECTS THE ELEGANCE OF BACH'S MUSIC.

J.S. Bach Chamber Music Hall

BY ZAHA HADID

Chamber music originated centuries ago as
a custom among the wealthy, who regularly
opened their homes and welcomed friends to join
them for an evening of intimate performances by
contemporary virtuosos. On a similar scale,
Zaha Hadid, working closely with an acoustician,
has brought back this personal music experience,
now enriched by her familiar zesty approach and
intriguing way with design. Within the confines
of the Manchester Art Gallery, Hadid and her
team fashioned an extraordinary space for the
sole purpose of highlighting the beautiful music
of Johann Sebastian Bach. Elegantly contrasting
with the subdued black background is an
acoustic fabric of translucent white, which wraps
effortlessly around a suspended steel frame.
Hadid: 'The design enhances the multiplicity of
Bach's work through a coherent integration of
formal and structural logic. A single continuous
ribbon of fabric swirls around itself, creating
layered spaces to cocoon the performers and
audience with an intimate fluid space.'

zaha-hadid.com

WORDS **JACLYN SPOKOJNY**
PHOTOS **LUKE HAYES**

Doppelturn-halle

BY ACKERMANN & RAFF

Ackermann & Raff's Oliver Braun fills us in on a gymnasium in southwest Germany, with a vibrant interior.

Project
The replacement of an old gym that was too small and in bad condition.

Problem
Integration of the gym, on its rather cramped building site, into a residential area where most buildings have no more than three floors.

Solution
We designed a building the same height as one with four standard floors, but our gym has three horizontal layers.

Exterior materials
Walls rise from a base of gabions, the central section is made from fibre-reinforced concrete, and the top is clad in a glass fibre textile membrane.

Interior materials
The 1210-m² floor has a PU coating, and we used latex paint – in green, yellow, orange and blue – for the walls and ceiling.

Colour
In contrast to the exterior, the interior concept features colours borrowed from contemporary art. We opted for a vibrant colour scheme to differentiate among rooms and functions.

ackermann-raff.de

WORDS **MEREL KOKHUIS**
PHOTOS **ZOOEY BRAUN**

BORING GYM CLASSES ARE PASSÉ AT HEILBRONN'S WARTBERGSCHULE, WHICH HAS A COLOURFUL NEW FACILITY BY ACKERMANN & RAFF.

SUPERNOVA

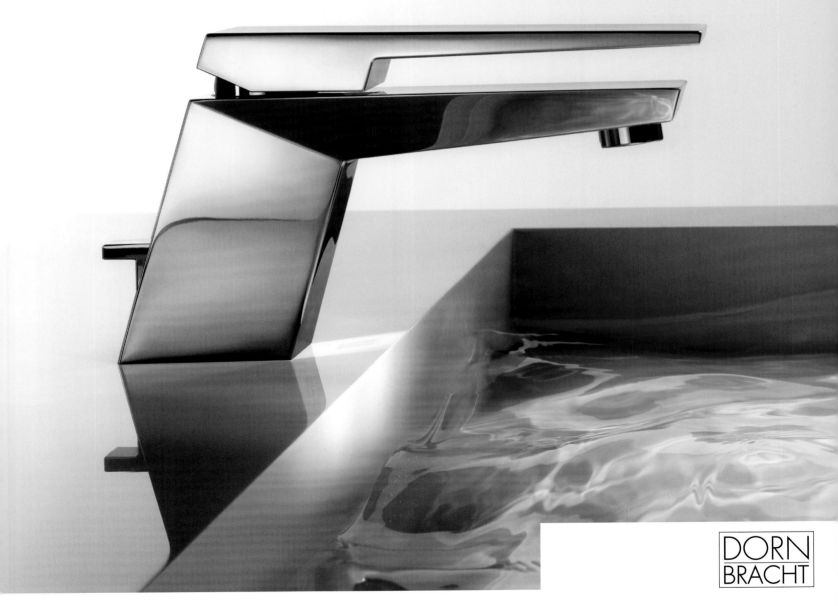

the SPIRIT *of* WATER

DORN BRACHT

A tap with sculptural qualities. A solitary unit that impresses its environment with ever changing reflections of objects and colours through its facets and polygonal surfaces. SUPERNOVA was created by Sieger Design. The SUPERNOVA brochure is available from **Aloys F. Dornbracht GmbH & Co. KG,** Köbbingser Mühle 6, D-58640 Iserlohn, Phone +49 (0) 2371 433-0, Fax +49 (0) 2371 433-232, E-Mail mail@dornbracht.de. **Dornbracht UK Ltd.,** Unit 8 & 9 Bow Court, Fletchworth Gate, Coventry CV5 6SP, Phone +44 (0) 2476-717129, Fax +44 (0) 2476-718907, E-Mail enquiries@dornbracht.co.uk. www.dornbracht.com

Choose the Original
Choose Success!

PHOTOS COURTESY OF PIA EDNIE-BROWN

DESIGN LAB PLASTIC FUTURES ASKS HOW WE WILL DESIGN, BUILD AND INHABIT THE URBAN ENVIRONMENT IN 2049.

Plastic Futures

BY PIA EDNIE-BROWN AND STUDENTS

What will life be like in 2049? According to Professor Pia Ednie-Brown of Australia's RMIT School of Architecture and Design, the answer lies in the distant past, some 3.6 billion years ago, when the earth's oldest form of architecture was the living 'thrombolite', a microbial rocklike structure. The professor and 12 of her students designed Plastic Futures, a fictional community based on their research of Mandurah and Lake Clifton, on the coast of Western Australia, where thrombolites are still found. Plastic Futures is one of five design labs collectively known as the Design Laboratory – an initiative that looks at how we can design, build and inhabit the urban environment in 2049. The project proposes that biotechnologies will be intertwined with digital innovation. 'We will need to adapt quickly to a rapidly altering global condition – climatically, economically, socially and technically,' says Ednie-Brown. 'We need to maximise our changeability and malleability.' The research culminated in an exhibition, showcased during the State of Design Festival in Melbourne. Polyester ceiling insulation dominated the space, while other malleable materials, such as crochet work, were used for their plastic properties.

designlaboratory.com.au

WORDS **KELLIE HOLT**
PHOTOS **TOBIAS TITZ**

UNIVERSITY OF AMSTERDAM LIBRARY, THE WORK OF IRA KOERS
AND ROELOF MULDER. PUBLISHED IN *FRAME* #71.
PHOTO COURTESY OF IRA KOERS AND ROELOF MULDER

THIRTY-FOUR FLAGS BEARING PORTRAITS OF CHINESE ORPHANS FLUTTER IN THE BREEZE THANKS TO BUILT-IN FANS IN THE FLAGPOLES.

Landscape of Childhood

BY YAN PEI-MING

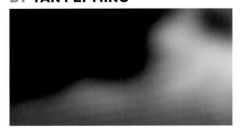

Known for monochrome portraits featuring traces of social and political conflict, Chinese artist Yan Pei-Ming painted orphans for the Ullens Center for Contemporary Art.

This is your first installation. What made you decide to work in the third dimension?
The main hall of the UCCA is gigantic – an absolutely sublime space, but very difficult to master. I had to organize the space without using partitions. I see this not as an installation but as a sort of *mise en scène* for paintings.

What's the mise en scène like?
To retain the transparency of the space, I hung poles from the ceiling and painted flags with a translucent quality. Embracing the paintings on opposite sides of the space are a large universal landscape and a monochrome

work in silver. I made ordinary portraits, but fans built into the poles move the flags and deform the images. The result is painting in motion.

Why the focus on portraiture?
I want to express human tragedy. When I saw orphans from the Beijing United Family Hospital, I asked myself, how it is possible to abandon a child? The families of these sick children are forced to leave them there, because they can't afford medical treatment. I wanted to express their fate.

ucca.org.cn

WORDS **FEMKE DE WILD**
PHOTOS **LIANG GUO, COURTESY OF UCCA**

POTS SHAPED LIKE LIFE-SIZE FIAT 500S ALLOWED TREES TO FLOURISH ALONG THE NORMALLY BARREN VIA MONTENAPOLEONE.

Per Fare un Albero

BY **FABIO NOVEMBRE**

Asked by Milan city council to enliven Via Montenapoleone, you planted trees in Fiat 500-shaped containers. Why?
Fabio Novembre: The street's two main problems are lack of greenery and illegal parking. It seemed natural to solve the two at the same time, merging them into the symbol of a new naturalism.

And the Fiat 500?
The obvious choice, as it's dear to us Italians. Fiat's enthusiasm for this project surprised me. It shows a new approach of the brand to communication. Brands are building new liquid nations based on taste.

Which means?
It seems to be a fascinating prospect, but in real life it's hard to handle. People start thinking of themselves as brands to be sold on the market. A client asks me to paint his portrait in my personal style. And if he's not particularly good-looking, he wants me to make him look better. I must admit that we designers risk building fake identities.

How about your own brand?
I'm a person, not a brand. Death could change me into a brand – but until then, let's just keep me as a name.

novembre.it

WORDS **JANE SZITA**
PHOTOS **COURTESY OF STUDIO NOVEMBRE**

14 by Omer Arbel

MARK

ANOTHER ARCHITECTURE

MARK Nº 23
DECEMBER 09 · JANUARY 10

WINNER GOLDEN CUBE
ART DIRECTORS CLUB
NEW YORK 2009
ADCAWARDS.ORG

KUMIKO INUI TOKYO · ALEXANDER BRODSKY MOSCOW · ZAHA HADID ROME · STEFANO BOERI LA MADDALENA · SEARCH & CHRISTIAN MÜLLER VALS · SOU FUJIMOTO TOKYO · IÑAKI DOMINGO & CARLA ARRANZ SOBRINI SÃO PAULO · CHIAKI ARAI OFUNATO · LETTER FROM SICHUAN · FAT LONDON · JENNY SABIN PHILADELPHIA

'Compromise is not a solution'

Explore Another Architecture

CULTURAL CENTRE AND LIBRARY IN OFUNATO, JAPAN BY CHIAKI ARAI PUBLISHED IN MARK Nº 23.
PHOTO **SERGIO PIRRONE**

MARK-MAGZINE.COM

SEIZURE, AN INSTALLATION BY ROGER HIORNS, RESULTED FROM A CHEMICAL PROCESS THAT COVERED A LONDON INTERIOR IN A MANTLE OF DEEP-BLUE CRYSTALS.

Seizure

BY ROGER HIORNS

It may have been ephemeral, but British artist Roger Hiorns' installation, *Seizure*, will probably go down in history as one of the more memorable and worthwhile contemporary art experiences on offer in the UK in the opening decade of the 21st century. Hiorns' cavernous Gothic fantasyland was created by pumping 75,000 litres of copper sulphate into an anonymous council flat in an abandoned 1950s' two-storey housing development in South London. Intensely blue crystals quickly grew over every surface–floors, walls, ceilings and a lone bathtub–transforming the bedsit into an ominous, odorous, slightly claustrophobic, encrusted grotto. For a few short weeks (until the block was demolished), a drab and unloved flat in a depressing and derelict inner-city development was given an unexpected and quite magical lease of life. Londoners and visitors alike made the pilgrimage to this deprived part of town in droves to experience the feat of chemistry and imagination.

artangel.org.uk

WORDS **GIOVANNA DUNMALL**
PHOTOS **MARCUS LEITH**

ATMOSPHERE, RATHER THAN REPRESENTATION, WAS THE AIM OF THIS STAGE SET, CONSISTING SOLELY OF 1000 LENGTHS OF 8-MM BEAD CHAIN.

Zone Nomadic

BY DORRELL GHOTMEH TANE

The stage set – or, as the architects prefer to call it, scenography – for *Zone Nomadic*, a performance piece by Japan's National Theatre and acclaimed dance company Noism, consists of the simplest of materials: 1000 suspended lengths of 8-mm bead chain, clustered in three shimmering rows. 'The space had to feel atmospheric rather than representational,' explains architect Tsuyoshi Tane, one of the three founding members of the international office Dorrell Ghotmeh Tane Architects, which created the set. 'It can appear or disappear in a flash, and lighting and movement give it a dynamic impact. This was important, since the performers don't belong to any specific time and place, and the music too spans all genres, from baroque

to pop.' Set off by the velvety black background, the bead chains variously suggest rain, light rays, curtains, ropes, webs and chains, depending on the lighting, movement and music – exactly the kind of kaleidoscopic effect the designers had in mind.

dgtarchitects.com

WORDS **IONA ROBERTS**
PHOTOS **TAKASHI SHIKAMA**

INTERNATIONAL FAIR-MARBLE TECHNOLOGIES DESIGN

CARRARA MARMOTEC 30° 2010

Carrara, Italy   Maggio_May, 19/22

PROMOSSO DA/PROMOTED BY:

INTERNAZIONALE
MARMI E MACCHINE
CARRARA SpA

ORGANIZZATO DA/ORGANIZED BY:

CARRARAFIERE
BUSINESS ON THE MOVE

Cassa
di Risparmio
di Carrara S.p.A.
SPONSOR UNICO BANCARIO
SOLE SPONSORING BANK

CON IL PATROCINIO DI/SUPPORTED BY:

Ministero
dello Sviluppo Economico

ISTITUTO NAZIONALE PER IL COMMERCIO ESTERO
ITALIAN INSTITUTE FOR FOREIGN TRADE

REGIONE
TOSCANA

TOSCANA
PROMOZIONE

AIPi

ADI ASSOCIAZIONE
PER IL DISEGNO
INDUSTRIALE

CarraraFiere Srl
Viale Galileo Galilei, 133

Tel +39 0585 787963

www.carraramarmotec.com

THE COMPLEX SPATIAL DESIGN OF THE SONGMAX STORE WAS INFLUENCED BY TRADITIONAL CHINESE GARDENS.

SongMax

BY ELEVATION WORKSHOP

For a showroom and prototype store featuring new women's clothing brand SongMax, New York- and Beijing-based design office Elevation Workshop was faced with an unpromising, low-ceilinged, 78-m² space. The solution, says designer Na Wei, was 'to focus on the transformation and transition of space through subtle and responsive material changes'. An L-shaped raised path through the interior evokes a catwalk or stage; grey-tiled pathways interwoven with this route create an intricate, knotlike organization of floor space. Vivid red rails running along three walls add to the lively perspectival effect, while a convertible fitting room doubles as a recessed 'display window'. CNC technology was used to fabricate resin panels and materials used for flooring, while thousands of beads were hand-strung to make the crystal curtain with its store-logo pattern. 'The spatial design is deeply influenced by traditional Chinese garden design, which has impressed me since childhood,' says Na Wei. 'I believe that poetic thinking is ingrained in Chinese culture.'

elevationworkshop.com

WORDS **JANE SZITA**
PHOTOS **JUN REN**

Mariscal Drawing Life

BY ESTUDIO MARISCAL

Design retrospectives can have the effect of transforming even the most vibrant body of work into a dull procession of museum pieces. Not so the recent Mariscal show at London's Design Museum, which took the magnificently messy form of a playful and seemingly impromptu installation by the Spanish designer himself. Entering the show through a tunnel of 640 drawings suspended from the ceiling, visitors were transported into Javier Mariscal's idiosyncratic graphic universe, in which even 3D objects appeared to have emerged fully formed from the designer's pen, as doodles made flesh. The lively orchestration of *New Yorker* covers, merchandising for the Barcelona Olympics, Camper for Kids packaging, the Villa Julia Playhouse, and a vast range of other works embodied Mariscal's exceptional linear vitality and unwavering optimism – an antidote to what he calls the 'immutable grey world' which 'has nothing to do with our dreams'.

mariscal.com

WORDS **JANE SZITA**
PHOTOS **COURTESY OF DESIGN MUSEUM LONDON**

THE INSTALLATION CELEBRATED THE IDIOSYNCRATIC GRAPHIC VITALITY OF JAVIER MARISCAL.

Goodbye & Hello

BY GEWERK DESIGN

TWO ELEMENTS FEATURED IN GEWERK DESIGN'S 380-M² GOODBYE & HELLO EXHIBITION: WHITE WOOD AND BLACK TAPE.

It was Dr Duncan MacDougall who attempted to weigh the human soul by placing dying patients on a scale and recording their weights before and after death. The average difference was 21 grammes. No one has ever duplicated his experiment. The exhibition Goodbye & Hello: Dialogue with the Beyond oscillated between the known and the unknown in terms of both content and design. Berlin-based Gewerk Design created the exhibition, which featured people's afterlife experiences, for the Museum of Communication in Bern. The setting was a fanciful white space lined in black stripes, which generated artificial perspectives, spatial illusions and bold contrasts that together influenced and disturbed the human sense of perception and orientation. 'Our design prepared visitors for stories and objects from an unknown and foreign place – the hereafter,' says Jens Imig of Gewerk Design. Goodbye & Hello received a 2009 iF communication design award and a nomination for the Design Preis Schweiz.

gewerk.com

WORDS **LILIA GLANZMANN**
PHOTOS **H. SAXER, COURTESY OF MUSEUM OF COMMUNICATION**

SENSE

ELEPHANT

THE ART & VISUAL CULTURE MAGAZINE

ISSUE №1

SÃO PAULO GUIDE

COLLAGE   BIKES & FASHION

ART & THE INTERNET

NEW TRENDS

STUDIO VISITS   UNIT PUBLISHING

PETER SAVILLE

FERNANDO GUTIÉRREZ

Launch issue price £12.99, €14.99, $19.99

WINTER 2009-10

**ELEPHANT, A NEW MAGAZINE ABOUT ART AND VISUAL CULTURE
ISSUE 1 OUT NOW • BY THE MAKERS OF FRAME
ELEPHANTMAG.COM**

PHOTO DIDIER PLOWY.

White Geology

BY PHILIPPE RAHM

The curators of La Force de l'Art 02, a triennial exhibition of contemporary art in France, asked architect Philippe Rahm to create a neutral, non-thematic space that would enable visitors to walk freely through the world of art without being overwhelmed by the setting. Inspired by the location, the nave of the Grand Palais in Paris, Rahm crafted White Geology, a bare ecosystem devoid of colour. He initially allocated an equal amount of space to each work of art displayed within the 125-x-24-m field of white parallelograms. In the manner of tectonic plates, however, these white elements 'shifted' – pushing and deforming the crisp white landscape as dictated by the dimensions of the work displayed and by the distance between an individual work and the viewer. White Geology reversed the idea of a conventional exhibition space by having the architecture adapt to the demands of the art rather than having the art adapt to the architecture.

philipperahm.com

WORDS **CHRIS SCOTT**
PHOTOS **COURTESY OF PHILIPPE RAHM**

EXPLORING THE POWER OF A WHITE SURFACE TO REFLECT LIGHT, RAHM CREATED AN INSTALLATION WITH A REFLECTION DEGREE OF 80 PER CENT.

FORMANI

CREATED BY **PIET BOON** DESIGN

THE CENTREPIECE OF THE FOCUSTERRA EXHIBITION, DESIGNED BY HOLZER KOBLER ARCHITECTS, IS A TOWER IN A COVERED COURTYARD.

focusTerra

BY HOLZER KOBLER

Geologists drill holes to learn about the earth's structure. Swiss scientists collect their findings in a remarkable way: focusTerra, a permanent exhibition at the Federal Institute of Technology Zürich, unites the existing collection of the Natural Sciences Institute with research carried out on site. When the Department of Earth Sciences moved into new premises, the covered courtyard of the renovated building was reserved for focusTerra. Its centrepiece is a tower that spirals up three levels nearly to the atrium skylight. 'Analogous to the forces below the earth's surface' is how architect Tristan Kobler describes the tower, whose smooth surface resembles an outcrop. Stairs lined with a ribbon of showcases connect the floors

and guide visitors through the layers of the earth. Holzer Kobler Architects not only curated the exhibited material in collaboration with the scientists involved, but also designed the entire venue, which was nominated for the Design Preis Schweiz. According to the report of the jury, which included Jasper Morrison, focusTerra is 'a good example of how design can respond effectively to a specific site'.

holzerkobler.ch

WORDS **LILIA GLANZMANN**
PHOTOS **JAN BITTER**

EACH CHAIR IN THE GARDEN-THEMED READING ROOM FEATURES A SEEDLING EMBROIDERED IN THICK, BLACK SHEEP'S WOOL.

CAC Reading Room

BY **ANOUK VOGEL, BART GULDEMOND AND JOHAN SELBING**

'A garden consists of many disparate elements that together form a whole,' says Anouk Vogel. 'We found that an interesting point of departure, and it resulted in an informal design.' In collaboration with Bart Guldemond and Johan Selbing, Vogel designed a new reading room for the Contemporary Art Centre (CAC) in Vilnius, Lithuania. The designers crafted asymmetric tables that, like the pieces of a puzzle, can be interconnected to form a continuous surface or used separately, depending on the occasion. Height-adjustable pendant lamps 'respond' to the arrangement of the tables. 'Like a garden,

the room can evolve – by adapting to different functions – from meeting room to reading room to exhibition space,' explains Vogel. 'Because most of the tables have more than four corners, we gave each more than four slender legs and added branches for increased stability.' Unfortunately, the birch forest they planned for the outdoor space will have to wait until the economic crisis is over.

anoukvogel.nl

WORDS **FEMKE DE WILD**
PHOTOS **JEROEN MUSCH**

MOBILE **BLACK EDITION**

ALU | MODULAR MERCHANDISING SYSTEMS
WWW.ALU.COM

MADEexpo

Milano Architettura Design Edilizia

Milan Fairgrounds, Rho, Italy, 03_06 February 2010

Build the Future!

MADE expo, the foremost trade fair with everything you need to create masterpieces of architecture and building construction

MADE expo is an initiative of:
MADE eventi srl
Federlegno Arredo srl

Organized by: MADE eventi srl
tel. +39 051 6646624 • +39 02 80604440
info@madeexpo.it • made@madeexpo.it

Promoted by:

ENCRYPT COLLECTION – THE CODE IS KEY

Encrypt is a sequence of codes as you'll see from the dotted patterns of
the Encode and Cypher ranges. From Morse Code and binary to dots and dashes …
The recycled content in the backing helps make this collection more sustainable.
This is a balanced collection that coordinates perfectly across styles.
A palette of vibrant, eye-catching colours gives you the ability
to create a lively atmosphere that's both fresh and modern.

PRODUCT: ENCRYPT COLLECTION, MENAGERIE
COLOUR: CYPHER CINNABAR, ENCODE CINNABAR, MENAGERIE MIDNIGHT

Interface **FLOR**

'Style is just the outside of content'
JEAN-LUC GODARD

FEATURES

PROJECTS IN PERSPECTIVE

WHAT'S THE BIG IDEA?

'An intuition that became an idea' is how STEVEN HOLL describes his new museum in Herning, Denmark. TOMAS SARACENO'S tangled webs and castles in the air originate in his notion of an idealized future world. Basing itself on one bold concept, a rural Irish home is a long, linear series of windows facing an empty landscape; while an equally bold Japanese house responds to urban density with a seemingly chaotic exploded floor plan. Meanwhile, MINISTRY OF DESIGN pays homage to 'ideas man' Leo Burnett with an ad-agency office that's strikingly cerebral.

ANY WAY THE WIND BLOWS

TOMAS SARACENO's poetic, lighter-than-air installations reflect a new way of life.

WORDS **FEMKE DE WILD**
PHOTOS **COURTESY OF TOMAS SARACENO**

MUSEO AERO SOLAR IS THE FIRST FLOATING MUSEUM MADE FROM A HUGE NETWORK OF PLASTIC BAGS (SEE AIR-PORT-CITY.ORG).

IN LUXEMBOURG, THE MUDAM MUSEUM RECENTLY PRESENTED THREE VIDEOS FEATURING *SPACE ELEVATOR II*, A WORK IN PROGRESS, CURRENTLY LOCATED IN ARGENTINA. COURTESY OF THE ARTIST, ANDERSENS CONTEMPORARY, TANYA BONAKDAR GALLERY AND PINKSUMMER CONTEMPORARY ART.

'People are travelling more and farther, and not all are confined to this planet'
TOMAS SARACENO

TOMAS SARACENO WAS BORN IN 1973 IN TUCUMAN, ARGENTINA. HE LIVES AND WORKS IN FRANKFURT AM MAIN.
PHOTO WOLFGANG GÜNZEL

Driven by ambition, fear or the hope for a better future, people search constantly for new places in which to live and for new forms of security. Argentine artist Tomas Saraceno puts his quest for alternatives into utopian spatial installations. His work is rooted in the tradition of superstructuralism, an architectural movement of the 1950s and '60s, but what Saraceno makes is less rational and rather more poetic. His visionary installations wrench themselves free of the earth, play with sunlight and gravity, and more often than not have a mesmerizing effect.

You were educated as an architect. What led you to study art?
The architecture I'd seen was pretty boring, and architects have to go after commissions and then try to please their clients. I wanted to develop new structures, but I saw few opportunities in architecture schools for experimental research. If there were more places with instructors like Peter Cook, who cofounded Archigram, I might have followed a different path. As it was, I felt better able to express my ideas through art.

And the concept of habitable floating environments?
That's a result of my lifestyle. Born in Argentina, I moved to Italy, returned to Argentina, left again for Europe – and travel is still a big part of my life. It would be great to have a studio that I could take along wherever I go. When I am in Berlin and in Frankfurt I really miss bright sunshine. A studio high above the clouds would always be filled with light. People today seem inclined to travel more and farther, and not all are confined to this planet.

Your work has obviously been influenced by superstructuralists like Cook and Yona Friedman.
That's right, also by Gyula Kosice, Farm and R.B. Fuller, but my work is much more mobile and far more flexible than Friedman's superstructures. I base my installations on clouds and on their organization into cloud constellations. Clouds grow, split apart, hang low, hover high, affect weather conditions and change as they approach cities. Studying the various types of clouds – nimbus, cumulus, cirrus and so on – is one way to generate >>>

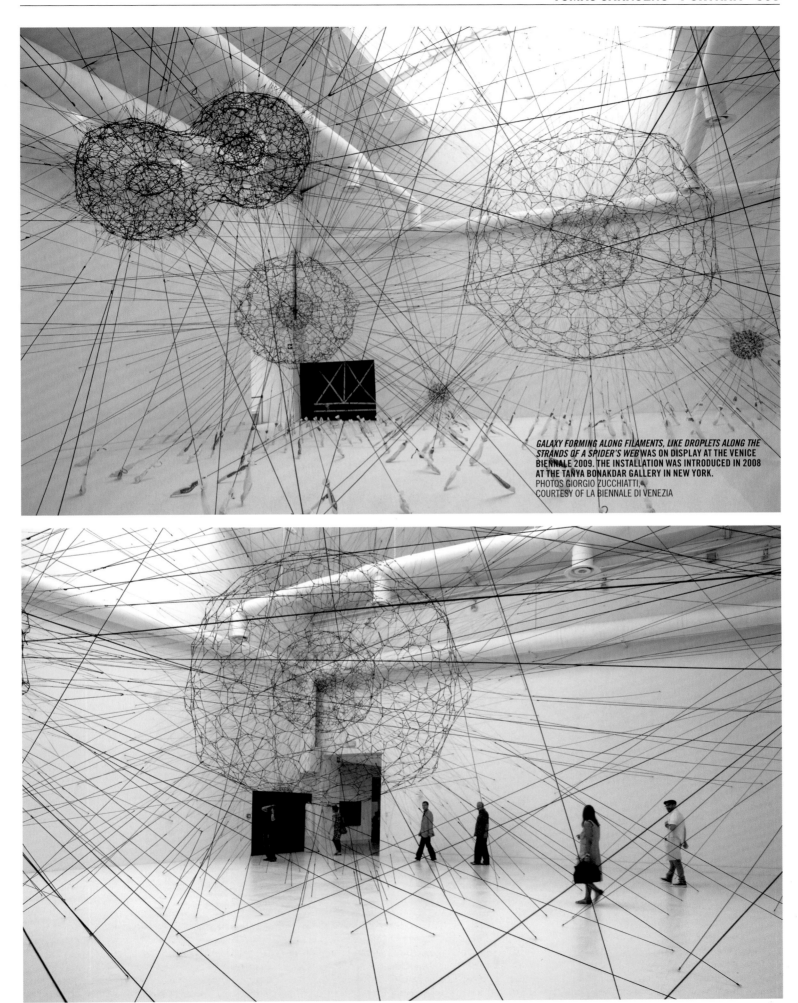

GALAXY FORMING ALONG FILAMENTS, LIKE DROPLETS ALONG THE STRANDS OF A SPIDER'S WEB WAS ON DISPLAY AT THE VENICE BIENNALE 2009. THE INSTALLATION WAS INTRODUCED IN 2008 AT THE TANYA BONAKDAR GALLERY IN NEW YORK.
PHOTOS GIORGIO ZUCCHIATTI,
COURTESY OF LA BIENNALE DI VENEZIA

SARACENO'S *BIOSPHERE MW 32/FLYING GARDEN/
AIR-PORT-CITY* APPEARED AT THE SHARJA BIENNIAL 8 IN 2007.
CREATED IN COLLABORATION WITH PINKSUMMER CONTEMPORARY ART.
PHOTO ROKMA

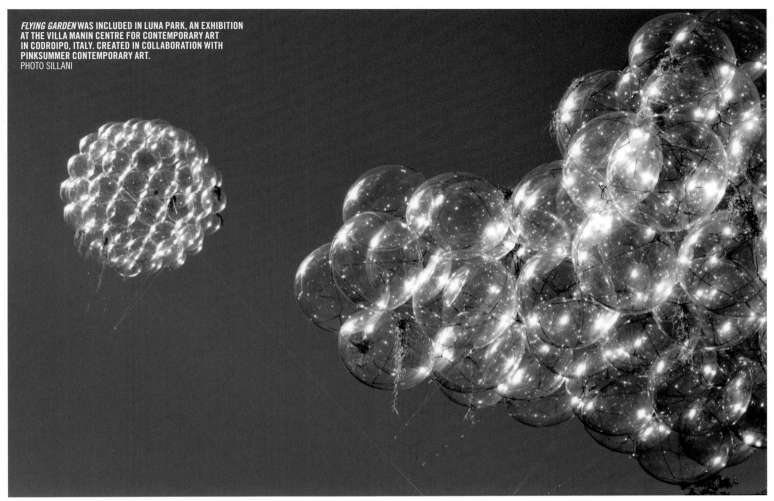

FLYING GARDEN WAS INCLUDED IN LUNA PARK, AN EXHIBITION AT THE VILLA MANIN CENTRE FOR CONTEMPORARY ART IN CODROIPO, ITALY. CREATED IN COLLABORATION WITH PINKSUMMER CONTEMPORARY ART.
PHOTO SILLANI

'We live on a spaceship; the earth floats constantly'

TOMAS SARACENO

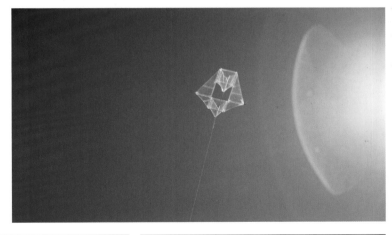

new ideas in architecture: imagine a kind of architecture that forms itself, that grows organically, that moves, that has no permanent location yet many options. New methods of architecture open new ways of looking at environmental issues. Much of the world's air pollution is caused by aeroplanes. Think what it would be like to travel in vehicles lighter than air.

What would these vehicles look like?
The premise is simple. Hot air is lighter than cold air, so when the sun heats the space inside a balloon, the balloon rises solely on the basis of solar energy. Contemporary travel relies on an enormous amount of power generated by fuels that damage the environment. I use the power of suspension. Floating modules can be connected to one another via a modular network and just as easily disconnected. Life in a floating structure necessitates extreme sensitivity to weather conditions and creates a much closer relationship between the occupant and the natural energy that propels the dwelling.

How do you feel about the relationship between people and nature?
Humans and nature are not separate territories; people are part of a complex system. In his ecosophy, Felix Guattari describes our world as an entity in which the social, environmental and mental worlds are inextricably interwoven.

Can you give us an example?
The *Museo Aero Solar* is a lighter-than-air vehicle – and the first floating museum – consisting of plastic bags attached to one another. It's already landed in ten locations. The structure uses only solar energy to fly. The project exists thanks to the cooperation of people at every stop who are invited to add plastic bags and help the museum grow. A city could be built in the same way.

How are photographs and video images used in your research?
Photos and videos allow us to see things that we can't picture mentally. Your brain can't capture as an image, for instance, the time necessary for the earth to move. The medium influences your powers of observation, and I allow natural phenomena to influence the medium, of course. My wind-based videos are >>>

THE ARTIST USED ELLIPTICAL HELIUM-FILLED PILLOWS, ELASTIC NETTING, TILLANDSIA PLANTS AND AIR TO MAKE *FLYING GARDEN/ AIR-PORT-CITY* (HERE AT SUDELEY CASTLE IN THE UK).

'Humans and nature are not separate territories'
TOMAS SARACENO

THE ENDLESS PHOTO WAS TAKEN AT SALAR DE UYUNI IN BOLIVIA, THE WORLD'S LARGEST SALT LAKE AND THE HIGHEST IN ALTITUDE. THE REFLECTION OF THE SKY BLURS THE HORIZON.

a good example; they're made by placing a sensor in the propeller of a wind turbine. The sensor sends signals to the camera, which makes more photos on a windy day than on a wind-still day. For *The Endless Photo*, we went to Bolivia to Salar de Uyuni, the largest salt lake – and the highest in altitude – in the world. The reflection of the sky on the smooth surface of the water absolutely blurs the horizon.

The installation you showed at the Venice Biennale was also based on the galaxy.
A recent theory postulates that right after the Big Bang, the newborn universe must have been a construction resembling a cobweb, and that the galaxies formed along its filaments, like dewdrops. Guided by this theory, we had a black widow spider spin her three-dimensional web in a miniature model of the exhibition space in Venice. We then made a duplicate of it many times greater. This year, after my studies at NASA, I submitted a proposal with a team for studying a three-dimensional cobweb in the microgravity environment of the ISS international space station. We discovered a method to actually scan a three-dimensional cobweb, so we can build an *exact* duplicate of it at the upcoming show in Bonniers Konsthall in Sweden this year.

Is there an interface between your work and reality?
Change is a lengthy process, but when people see new possibilities, they inevitably elaborate on them. Times will change. It used to be that water – oceans and rivers – determined how people organized their lives. When we learned how to travel without using water, it influenced how and where we built our settlements. What's more, the notion of a floating vehicle isn't as far-fetched as you might think it is. We live on a spaceship.

And art is the best medium?
You're searching for answers, but it's the questions themselves that are most interesting. Architects have to have all the answers, but art is more flexible. Olafur Eliasson once said the same thing in an interview in your magazine (see *Frame* 49, page 69). Art can be used to open people's minds and to alter perception. Art forces you to reflect and demands that you reposition yourself. ■

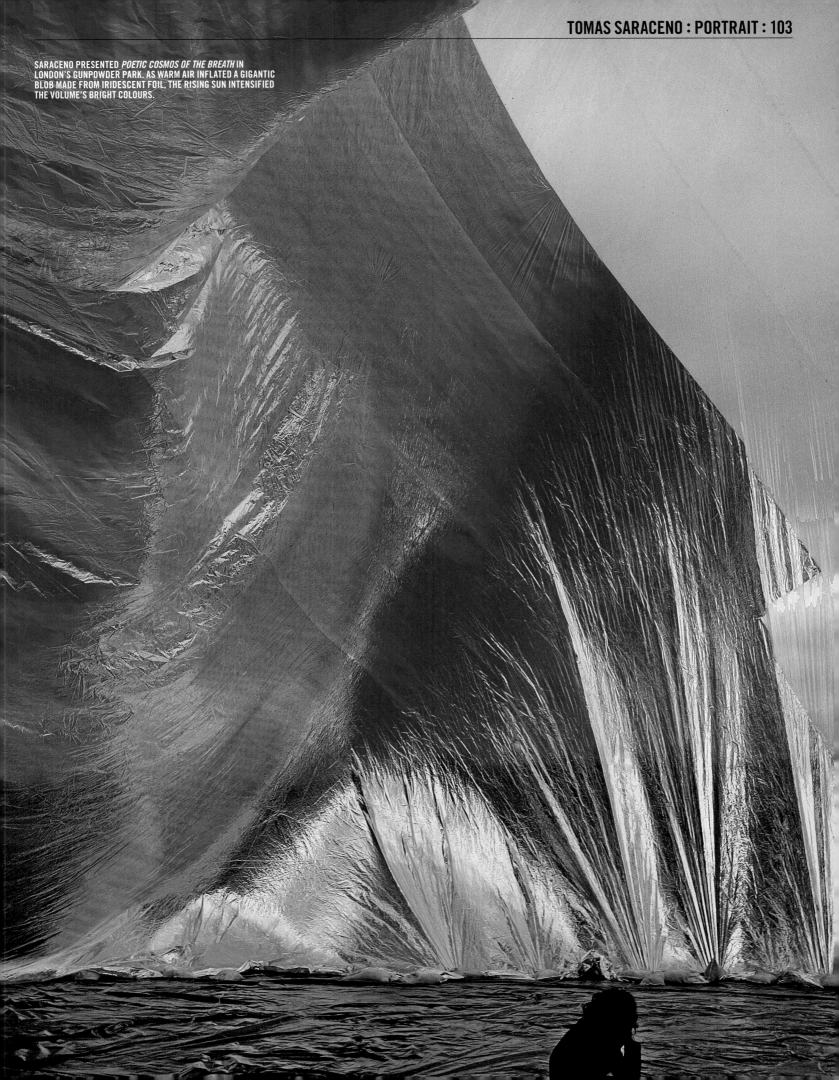

SARACENO PRESENTED *POETIC COSMOS OF THE BREATH* IN LONDON'S GUNPOWDER PARK. AS WARM AIR INFLATED A GIGANTIC BLOB MADE FROM IRIDESCENT FOIL, THE RISING SUN INTENSIFIED THE VOLUME'S BRIGHT COLOURS.

CARTE BLANCHE ET ROUGE

Two new CAMPER stores based on the 'Together' concept opened recently. Let's take a look at some background information.

WORDS **MEREL KOKHUIS**
WITH THE COOPERATION OF CHRIS SCOTT
PHOTOS **COURTESY OF CAMPER**

What do you make of the love affair between Spanish shoe label Camper and all those product designers – a list that includes Jaime Hayon, Alfredo Häberli, the Bouroullecs, Konstantin Grcic, the Campanas, Tokujin Yoshioka and Hella Jongerius? Wouldn't a footwear brand be better off working with fashion designers or, at the very least, designers who specialize in interiors rather than in products? Camper's Philippe Salva answers in the negative. 'Camper's always associated its collections more with design than with fashion. According to the founder of Camper, shoes are more about industrial design than about fashion. What's more, we love a challenge and the discovery of new areas of work. Our shops have always been our most important means of communication. The first Camper stores – most of which were designed by Fernando Amat – had an identical appeal. As our self-confidence grew, we dared to express the unique aspects of Camper – contradiction, diversity, simplicity, functionality and, above all, fun, fantasy and positivity – in our stores, as visualized by various designers.' Camper's requests are virtually nonexistent. Each designer is free to put his or her own stamp on the shop. As long as the logo colours – red and white – appear in the design, the result is a happy Camper. The selection process, says Salva, is intuitive. 'We don't have a predetermined plan. When we meet a designer and it clicks, we look into the possibility of working together. All we expect from these designers is a strong sense of creativity and a real connection between them and the Camper brand.' ▬▬

THANKS TO TOKUJIN YOSHIOKA'S BOUQUET CHAIRS, A CUSTOMER
TRYING ON SHOES AT CAMPER LONDON FEELS LIKE CINDERELLA —
OR THE PRINCE!

CAMPER STORE IN LONDON
BY TOKUJIN YOSHIOKA

What piques your curiosity on hearing that
a Japanese designer created a London shop
for a Spanish footwear brand? You're interested
in how the store expresses the various
nationalities involved. Do we see the designer's
Japanese roots, does the place have a Spanish
flair or is the store an example of Britain's retail
culture? Designer Tokujin Yoshioka says: none
of the above. 'When Camper asked me to
design a shop, I had no clue as to its location.
So I pitched a universal concept. And practically
everything I proposed exists in the completed
interior.' Yoshioka used his Bouquet chairs for
Moroso in three colourways. He panelled a nearby
wall in even more fabric flowers and crafted
displays from his well-known ice-crystal material.
A minor intervention, a major impact and a
design bearing the familiar Yoshioka signature.

PHOTO COURTESY OF STUDIO BOUROULLEC

CAMPER STORE IN PARIS BY RONAN AND ERWAN BOUROULLEC

In the shadow of the Centre George Pompidou, Camper has just opened its third Paris store. Part of the Camper Together concept, the shop is the work of Ronan and Erwan Bouroullec, who were also responsible for a recently completed Camper store in Copenhagen. The new Paris store has the unmistakable stamp of the Bouroullecs, which makes it stand out in this vibrant area of the city. The designers employed a palette of reds and oranges, which complement Camper's familiar company colours, and selected furniture from their Steelwood collection for Magis. The result, enhanced by tactile panels of quilted fabric throughout the shop, is an inviting and open atmosphere. The interior successfully combines two of Camper's top priorities: design and function.

PHOTO COURTESY OF STUDIO BOUROULLEC

PHOTO MURACCIOLE ANSORG

PHOTO COURTESY OF STUDIO BOUROULLEC

MUSEUM PIECES

FIVE new museum spaces in five different countries. FOUR collections on show for the first time. THREE radical renovations of old interiors. TWO purpose-built architectural landmarks. ONE museum that's also home to an art collector. ZERO compromise in terms of design values.

THE INTERIOR IS STRIPPED DOWN TO AN ARCHITECTURAL SKELETON, WITH NEW ELEMENTS KEPT SIMPLE AND INDUSTRIAL.

IN THE MUDE

In its new incarnation as MUDE Lisbon, a former bank building becomes an intimate, informal space for visitors to experience fashion and design, courtesy of RCJV ARCHITECTS.

WORDS **JACLYN SPOKOJNY**
PHOTOS **LEONARDO FINOTTI**

Formerly the workaday anchor of Lisbon's city centre, the 57-year-old Banco Nacional Ultramarino building, designed by modernist architect Cristino da Silva, has undergone a transformation that could easily ignite a full-on revitalization of the area. In a quick sequence of events, the Lisbon City Council acquired the vacant, dilapidated building and handed the creative licence to architects Ricardo Carvalho and Joana Vilhena of RCJV Architects, who were charged with the daunting task of converting a building the size of an entire city block –described as a 'modern ruin' – into an interesting museum.

In its new incarnation as MUDE: Design and Fashion Museum, the former bank was to reveal the inner workings of fashion and design so often hidden from view. In addition, visitors would view original designs scarcely available to the general public. Recognizing the beauty that once existed in a building erected more than half a century ago, the architects aimed for an intervention that would strike a balance between reinvigorating the old structure and implementing an innovative and experimental programme.

The latter was the result of the building having been stripped of its interior walls many years ago, an act that inspired RCJV to retain the clear, unobstructed layout. Further adding to the architects' open-plan strategy were the building's unique views of the Baixa Pombalina, the 18th-century city centre planned by the Marquis of Pombal following the earthquake of 1755. According to Carvalho and Vilhena, it's only inside this building that you can see an entire block of the Baixa.

The architects defined the wall-less spaces by means of a strategic lighting plan. 'We used light, both natural and artificial, to design the space,' says Carvalho.The bright-white, illuminated rubber screens that encase the lift core, the stairways and the interior of the vast counter create an interesting visual contrast to the dark concrete ceilings and columns. Carvalho and Vilhena also designed a screen that unifies the surroundings through its placement – along the perimeter walls of the building – while permitting natural light to enter the space and visitors to look out on the urban vista. 'From the windows, you can see the street and watch people passing by. We wanted to keep the visual relation with the city.'

Apart from the addition of an impressive lighting system, the architects approached >>>

WHITE DIAPHANOUS CURTAINS COVER THE NUMEROUS WINDOWS AND ENSURE A UNIFORM VISUAL EXPERIENCE.

'Putting functions together allows us to discover new relations among them'

RICARDO CARVALHO

BRIGHT WHITE LIGHTING LIFTS THE HEAVY INDUSTRIAL EFFECT.

the restoration as an exacting exercise in restraint – the basis of the entire project, from the outset. 'The museum is not small, and the budget was modest,' says Vilhena. 'We invested in artificial light and in the consolidation of the destroyed building, mainly with new concrete slabs and pavements. We used compressed-air sandblasting on the ceiling. Ours was a surgical intervention performed mostly on the framework, however, which was riddled with safety problems. It had numerous holes, loose cables and so forth.'

Having survived a former order to demolish the building, the large counter that dominates the main floor – the final remnant of the original bank building and what Carvalho calls 'the only relevant element of the original project' – was minimally altered by the addition of white screening to enhance the ambience created by the artificial lighting it conceals.

Another, subtler theme that influences circulation emerged from RCJV's theory of materiality. Because the designers were steadfast in their desire to minimize the number of interventions made, they allowed existing materials to satisfy their ideal of a comfortable, casual environment. This notion was critical to the architects, who defined the architecture by envisioning a construction site. Says Vilhena: 'We would like people to have an informal relationship with the sophisticated pieces on display. Our project revolves around the idea of a work in progress – we believe this is relevant to the atmosphere of a contemporary design museum.' Examples of their construction-site mentality are pallets used to display the work, Tyvek fabric in the cafeteria, exposed lighting, bare shelving and a new industrial paving material used for roads: the white surface is made from crushed glass.

The building pays homage to its past, in the form of structural bones for all to see, while simultaneously ensconcing itself in the design vernacular of the 21st century. MUDE welcomes visitors into a relaxed, industrial environment that helps them to bond with the exhibits, thus truly heightening the 'user experience'. As Ricardo Carvalho puts it, 'What we built is an informal space that combines designs, works of art, concerts, lectures, a bookshop and a cafeteria. Putting functions together allows us to discover new relations among them.' ■

A FLOWING SENSE OF SPACE WAS CREATED BY REMOVING THE WALLS INSTALLED IN THE PREVIOUS, UNSUCCESSFUL REMODELLING.

'We'd like people to have an informal relationship with the sophisticated pieces on display'
JOANA VILHENA

BANISTERS AND MARBLE FLOORING SURVIVE IN THE ENTRANCE HALL.

THE EXHIBITS ARE DISPLAYED ON PALLETS, IN KEEPING WITH THE ROUGH-AND-READY THEME.

PROJECT NAME MUDE - Museum of Design and Fashion of Lisbon.
DESIGNER Ricardo Carvalho + Joana Vilhena Arquitectos
WEBSITE rcjv.com
LOCATION Rua Augusta 24, Lisbon, Portugal
CLIENT MUDE and Lisbon City Council.
MATERIALS Industrial materials like concrete and steel
CONSTRUCTION Canas Correia
TOTAL FLOOR AREA 2,634 m²
STAR PIECE Gio Ponti's Arabesco table
TYPICAL VISITOR A wide range of people of varying age and professions
NUMBER OF VISITORS PER YEAR 65 000,00 since the opening in late May 2009
UPCOMING EXHIBITION It is Forbidden to Forbid - Design in the 1960s and 70s
PERMANENT EXHIBITION The collection (design items)
SPECIALISATION Design: furniture and fashion

LIGHT POURS INTO THE GALLERY THROUGH GLAZING THAT UNITES THE CURVED CEILING WITH THE ROOF PLANE.

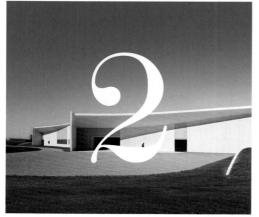

THE HOLL TRUTH

In his new museum for the Danish city of Herning, STEVEN HOLL creates a perfect, and almost metaphysical, balance of past, present, curvilinear and rectilinear.

WORDS **JACLYN SPOKOJNY**
PHOTOS **ROLAND HALBE**

A building that is just as interesting when viewed from above as it is when one moves through the space is a rarity. Such is the case with Steven Holl's new centre for the arts in the Danish city of Herning. A city relatively unheard of before the mid-1960s was projected onto the world stage thanks to an unrivalled collection of art by Italian artist Piero Manzoni, famous for the role he played in the Arte Povera movement. Important art pieces, however, do not just land on the doorsteps of museums in obscure places like Herning. Acquisitions of this calibre are more often obtained through generous endowments or, in unique circumstances, through the artist's personal donation to a museum's collection.

Having formed a bond with the owners of Angli, a local shirt factory, Manzoni made just such a donation. Initially his work was displayed in the converted factory, which evolved into a landmark art museum that is currently, however, no more than a relic of the past. Across the street is its incarnation, a structure designed by architect Steven Holl that is equal parts past, present, curvilinear and rectilinear.

This wonderful combination can be attributed to Holl's desire to 'anchor the architecture to the specific site and programme'. His influence here was the original factory, shaped like a shirt collar, which prompted him to picture the silhouette of a shirt as the framework for his design. Choosing the sleeve as the visual allusion and overall concept for the museum, he says that, seen from an aerial perspective, the building 'resembles a pile of shirtsleeves'. Referring to his concept as a 'heuristic device to open into the design problem', Holl adds that

the heart of this project was an 'intuition that became an idea which, in turn, holds the manifold parts of the architecture together'. Delving even deeper into the architect's thoughts, we find that the museum 'is not really about shirtsleeves at all – if you experience the space and light, you feel something special'.

The renowned architect certainly makes it difficult to disagree with him. Upon entering the galleries, you are completely enveloped in natural light – light that, at first glance, appears to be emanating from the walls themselves but is, in fact, seeping through the glazing that unites the convex curves of the ceiling, with their corresponding roof planes.

Having honed his ability to illuminate spaces over years of practice and experimentation, Holl stresses his refusal to compromise on one >>>

CHARACTERIZING THE INTERIOR OF THE MUSEUM IS AN ABUNDANCE
OF NATURAL LIGHT, WHICH GENTLY REFLECTS OFF THE SOFTLY
CURVED FORMS OF THE TWO-WAY TRUSS CEILING.

ALTHOUGH NOT IMMEDIATELY APPARENT TO VISITORS, THE HERNING CENTRE OF THE ARTS BOASTS AN ENERGY-SAVING GEOTHERMAL COOLING SYSTEM.

Holl describes the project as 'intuition that became an idea'

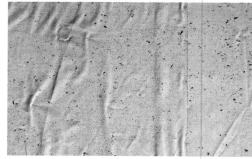

thing when designing a museum. He expresses the need for orthogonal walls in gallery spaces with an interesting anecdote: 'Years ago, while designing the interior spaces of the Kiasma Museum in Helsinki, I reviewed the model and drawings with several artists, including Vito Acconi, James Turrell and Richard Nonas. I remember Nonas exclaiming, "Steven, the floor must meet the wall in a right angle. My art work must have this simple geometry!"'

By no means do perpendicular gallery walls make Holl a 'square' designer. All it takes is a stroll across the museum's site to realize that Holl is a master when it comes to understanding how and when to manipulate the rigour of the line. 'This site is in the centre of the flat land of the Jutland Peninsula. Responding to the land expanse was one of the first impulses

of the design. Curved mounds turn to protect and create space on the street side and extend outward toward the horizon on the south side. It is a fusion of architecture and landscape.'

The drama generated by the integration of site and building converges at the entrance to the museum. 'When you enter the building, the dynamic of curved light and space is unveiled in overlapping perspectives. A feeling of surprise after the calm exterior engages the visitor.' Perhaps the best part of the design is Holl's ability to get visitors involved with the interior of the museum while also elevating Herning's status from international art scene to international architecture scene. ■

PROJECT NAME HEART Herning Museum of Contemporary Art
DESIGNER Steven Holl Architects, New York
WEBSITE stevenholl.com
LOCATION Birk Centerpark 8, DK-7400 Herning, Denmark
CLIENT HEART Foundation
MATERIALS Steel, concrete, glass
CONSTRUCTION c.c. contractor
TOTAL FLOOR AREA 5,500 m²
DANISH ARCHITECT Kjær & Richter
LANDSCAPE ARCHITECT Schönherr Landskab
STAR PIECE Socle du Monde, 1961, by Piero Manzoni (HEART Collection)
TYPICAL VISITOR Cultural tourist
NUMBER OF VISITORS PER YEAR 40,000
UPCOMING EXHIBITION Indian Highway (30.01.2010-24.05.2010) Socle du Monde 2010 (16.10.2010-23.01.2011)
PERMANENT EXHIBITION HEART Collection including works by Piero Manzoni, Lucio The Macura Museum Fontana, Paul Gadegaard, John Kørner, Troels Wörsel and others
SPECIALISATION Contemporary Art

SEVENTEEN

THE CURVES OF THE CEILING WORK IN PERFECT HARMONY WITH
THE RIGIDITY OF PERPENDICULAR WALLS IN THE GALLERY SPACES.

RUDOLF STINGEL'S PAINTINGS, *UNTITLED* , 2008,
IN THE CENTRAL COURTYARD.

VENETIAN CLASS

In his extraordinary renovation of
the stately Punta della Dogana in Venice,
TADAO ANDO pointedly omitted the
one thing that all contemporary exhibition
spaces share: white walls.

WORDS **JAN-WILLEM POELS**
PHOTOS **ORCH (ORSENIGO_CHEMOLLO)**

Every other year the art world flocks to
the Venice Biennale to check out the latest
in contemporary art. One of great pleasures
of viewing art in Venice is the experience offered
by the diverse settings in which the shows are
held. In addition to the many national pavilions
at the Gardini, visitors can explore countless
exhibitions in palazzos, churches, private homes
and warehouses all over the old city. This year,
a spectacular venue has been added to the
itinerary: the Punta della Dogana.

This monumental building, which once
housed a maritime customs house, occupies the
tip of Dorsoduro Island, at the junction of the
Grand and Giudecca Canals. Although part of the
building dates as far back as the 15th century,
what we see today is largely a 17th-century
structure. The building had fallen into serious

disrepair in recent decades, before becoming
the subject of a competition for its
redevelopment. Winning the competition
on the basis of his proposal to transform the
building into a centre of contemporary art was
a Frenchman, François Pinault, who owns an
immense art collection. Having successfully
collaborated with Tadao Ando on the renovation
of another Venetian landmark, the Palazzo
Grassi, Pinault unsurprisingly opted to partner
with Ando on the Punta della Dogana project
as well. The Japanese architect – a master of
renovations that respect the original architecture
of a building – has worked on a number
of handsome museum spaces, nearly always
realized within a very short, un-Italian time span
of two years or less. The rational, triangular
structure of the Dogana corresponds

to the shape of the island tip on which it stands.
The interior is composed of long rectangular
spaces separated by a series of parallel walls
that run perpendicular to the canals.

The layout of the exhibition spaces extends
from the entrance on the side of the building
near the steps of the Church of Santa Maria della
Salute to a spectacular opening that faces the
St Marks Basin. Here, a specially commissioned
sculpture, *Boy with Frog* by American artist
Charles Ray, forms the building's exclamation
mark. The nude child can be read as an
allegory for the curiosity of artists but hardly
as a contemporary David: this is no heroic
giant slayer.

Tadao Ando re-created the original interior
by removing all partitions that were added
during previous renovations. His immaculate >>>

THE FIRST EXHIBITION SPACE WITH RACHEL WHITEREAD'S *UNTITLED (ONE HUNDRED SPACES)*, 1995, ON THE FLOOR. ON THE WALL (FOREGROUND) IS A PAINTING BY LUC TUYMANS; THE HORSE IN THE BACKGROUND IS MAURIZIO CATALAN'S *UNTITLED*. AT THE BACK OF THE ROOM, FELIX GONZALES-TORRES' CURTAIN-LIKE *UNTITLED (BLOOD)*, 1992, MARKS THE ENTRANCE TO THE SPACE.

HUANG YONG PING'S *A FOOTBALL MATCH OF JUNE 14TH, 2002,* ECHOES THE CLASSICAL PROPORTIONS OF THE GROUND FLOOR.

'I aimed for the design of spaces in which raw materials enter into a dialogue, which I believe enriches the appreciation of the art'
TADAO ANDO

IN THE FOREGROUND: FISCHLI & WEISS, *UNTITLED (TREE STUMP),* 2005, A CAST POLYURETHANE SCULPTURE.

work included the exposure of ancient brick walls and original wooden roof trusses. The historical presence of the building is felt throughout the building, in every nook and cranny. Most of the new additions – such as floors, cores for electrical and mechanical systems, and staircases leading to first-floor galleries – are made from smooth, polished concrete. Ando has called concrete the 'marble of contemporary architecture', and his use of the material has become a trademark of his buildings. Here in Venice, he needed highly skilled workers to achieve the desired colour and texture of the poured-concrete floors and walls.

Ando enriched his balance of old and new elements in the Dogana building with subtle details. One example is the replacement of openings on the ground floor, towards the canal, with new windows that provide museum visitors with magnificent views of the city. To eliminate possible reflections that might interfere with the safety of boats navigating the canals, Ando had steel window screens made according to traditional Venetian metalworking methods. The screens are a direct quotation of Venetian architect Carlos Scarpa, who used similar screens in his famous interior design of the Olivetti shop on the San Marco Square.

Another example of Ando's meticulous attention to detail are brown air-conditioning ducts in the main galleries, which thanks to their colour blend in nicely with the wooden beams and trusses of the roof, while also housing spotlights that remove the need for separate spots. Ando's biggest architectural gesture was the insertion of a 'concrete box' over two bays in the centre of the space. A reversal of roles occurs in this large, square, double-height room, where the poured-concrete walls are new and the floor is made from *masegni*, the traditional slab stones used to pave the streets of Venice. Here Francesco Bonami and Allison Gingeras, the curators of the current show, Mapping the Studio, have displayed pieces that complement the design of the space: four huge Rudolf Stingel paintings, one on each wall.

Three rather abstract works feature a fence pattern, while a more realistic painting depicts a blown-up image of the young Stingel's army ID card. The subtle grey tones in these paintings conform to Ando's shiny concrete walls in terms of both colour and severity. This brings us to the question of how well the current form of the building supports its function as a space for Pinault's collection of contemporary art. >>>

THE CENTRAL COURTYARD, WITH ITS CONCRETE
WALLS AND A MASEGNI FLOOR, DISPLAYS RUDOLF
STINGEL *UNTITLED (ALPINO, 1976)*, 2006.

JAKE AND DINOS CHAPMAN'S *FUCKING HELL* LOOKS
AS IF IT WERE ALMOST DESIGNED TO FIT BENEATH
THE ANCIENT WOODEN BEAMS.

SECOND-FLOOR SPACE WITH CINDY SHERMAN WORKS ON THE WALL AND A JEFF KOONS SCULPTURE IN THE FOREGROUND: *BOURGEOIS BUST - JEFF AND ILONA*, 1991

'Concrete is the marble of contemporary architecture'
TADAO ANDO

CHARLES RAY'S RELIEF, *LIGHT FROM THE LEFT*, 2007, AND A MAGICAL LAGOON VIEW FROM ONE OF THE HALF-MOON WINDOWS OF THE SECOND FLOOR.

'Since the Punta della Dogana is a special, characteristic place,' says Ando, 'I aimed for the design of spaces in which raw materials enter into a dialogue, which I believe enriches the appreciation of the art.' The beauty of the building and its renovation is not in doubt, although the results are a tad too perfect for my taste: the space feels slick. But what I find most striking is what's missing from the building: white walls. Normally a must in any contemporary art museum, the white wall is nowhere to be found in the Dogana's exhibition spaces.

Most of the art currently on display is overwhelmed by the presence of the building. The wood-framed, brown-toned Sigmar Polke paintings, mounted on metal stands, fade into the brick walls to become part of the building. And instead of being blown away

at the horrors depicted in the tabletop tableau of plastic figurines that feature in Jake and Dinos Chapman's *Fucking Hell*, one marvels at how well the wood-and-glass display cases containing these scenes relate to the beams overhead. Even the strongest contemporary art risks becoming merely decorative in these interiors. And, as seen in the main room, the curators actually selected works meant to match the architecture.

Although Ando's architectural language is understated, he did nothing to hide or soften the historical presence of the original building or to create restrained spaces that would give the art on display a more neutral backdrop. Ando has produced an environment that makes for an interesting clash between architecture and art.

PROJECT NAME Punta della Dogana
DESIGNER/ARCHITECT Tadao Ando
WEBSITE andotadao.org
LOCATION Venice, Italy
CLIENT François Pinault Foundation
MATERIALS brick (renovations), tiles (roof renovation), wood (roof beam renovation), concrete (new building elements)
CONSTRUCTION renovation 2008 - 2009
TOTAL FLOOR AREA 5,000 m²
STAR PIECE *Boy with Frog* from Charles Ray, specially commissioned for museum
NUMBER OF VISITORS 8,000 per week since the museum opened in June
CURRENT EXHIBITION (no closing date announced as of yet): 'Mapping the Studio', curated by Alison Gingeras & Francesco Bonami
SPECIALISATION contemporary art from collection of François Pinault

GREY WALLS ENHANCE THE BRUTALIST ATMOSPHERE OF THE BUILDING, WHICH IS KEEPING WITH SERBIAN'S COMMUNIST HISTORY AS PART OF THE FORMER YUGOSLAVIA.

PRIVATE VIEW

VLADIMIR MACURA lives in the museum he founded to house his personal collection of 20th-century art.

WORDS **IONA ROBERTS**
PHOTOS **ANA KOSTIC**

Walking through the Macura Museum, in its spectacular location on the Danube some 10 km from Belgrade, you get the feeling that you've stumbled into someone's home. And that's because you have. Vladimir Macura, whose collection the museum houses, lives on the premises for part of the year. You can stroll through the rooms he inhabits, study the posters on his bathroom walls, flip through his books, and otherwise enjoy a vicarious insight into his life. Voyeurism adds an extra dimension to the museum, where notable works of modern art are displayed alongside significant pieces of furniture, and both are interwoven with documentation and the ordinary detritus of everyday life. It's impossible to forget what most museums are eager to disguise: that these objects are an arbitrary and subjective

collection and not an assemblage based on some objective canon.

Arguably, Vladimir Macura's museum tells you as much about the man as it does about the works on show. He's often on hand to give his guests a guided tour. 'The number of visitors is not important,' he replies when asked about statistics. 'What does matter is that people usually come because the museum has been recommended to them. We don't do any marketing at all.' The Macura is a viral museum, and its design clearly illustrates that fact.

Architects Nenad Katic and Ivan Kucina, who call the museum 'a mutant design' and 'a very successful failure', were first contacted by Macura to design a small gallery, about 180 m², to be built on a site close to Novi Banovci, a place not far from the Serbian capital.

The mini-labyrinthine floor plan they devised to maximize wall space reminded the client of a Julio Knifer meander painting in his collection, and a more ambitious plan started taking shape. Returning to the architects, Macura now asked for a museum – five times the size of the gallery, with an additional storey – that would include a café and an apartment, in which he would live part of the time, as well as exhibition space.

The architects designed and presented their plan. 'But it would be a year later before we were contacted again and invited to look at the building,' says Katic, 'which was already in the final stages of construction!' Macura had gone ahead and built the museum, changing the design where he saw fit. The architects' plan for two external staircases to the roof, for example, had become a pair of glazed atria. >>>

HOMELY CLUTTER PREVAILS IN MANY PARTS OF THE MUSEUM-CUM-HOME.

The architects call the building 'a mutant design' and 'a very successful failure'

THE MUSEUM-HOME'S OWN BEACH, ON THE SHORES OF THE DANUBE.

'We were greatly disappointed by the changes made to the original design,' says Kucina. 'Initially, we believed these alterations had diminished the architectural value of the building. However, unexpectedly positive feedback from the Serbian cultural community made us reconsider our attitude. New value emerges when a work of architecture ceases to be only an object and becomes an instrument of social interaction – as here, when the client became a coauthor of the design. The process reflects new developments in participative design methodology, although what happened at Novi Banovci was unplanned and spontaneous.'

Once the museum had been completed and the exhibits displayed, the architects found the final result 'charming', says Katic.

'The architecture and the presence of the client's home underline the impression of informality, immediacy and freedom that is so crucial to experiencing and understanding the art on display. The banality and rawness of the materials used in the interior form an ideal, contrasting backdrop for a collection of outstanding art.' The Macura Museum effectively deprofessionalizes architecture in much the same way that it deprofessionalizes the museum collection itself. The result is an antidote to the often sterile and commercial art-gallery environment – a significant statement in light of the Macura's status as the first designated museum built in Serbia since the Belgrade Museum of Modern Art was erected in 1964. ∎

PROJECT NAME Macura Museum
DESIGNERS Ivan Kucina and Nenad Katic, architects; Vladimir Macura, art collector
LOCATION Novi Banovci, Serbia
CLIENT Vladimir Macura
MATERIALS Concrete frame, brick walls, aluminium window frames, plastered interior walls, exposed concrete floors
CONSTRUCTION 2008
TOTAL FLOOR AREA 800 m²
TYPICAL VISITOR Lover of art, architecture, nature and scenic views
PERMANENT EXHIBITION Art and documentation from the former Yugoslavia, such as Zenitism, Nadrealism and Yugo-Dada from the 1920s and '30s; work done by the Gorgona Group in the '60s and '70s; and furniture and design from the '50s and '60s
SPECIAL FEATURE The collection of Vladimir Macura

THE SIMPLE LINES OF THE BUILDING AND UNFINISHED CONCRETE
FORM AN EFFECTIVE CONTRAST WITH THE WORKS ON SHOW, WHICH
REPRESENT SOME OF THE BEST EXAMPLES OF MODERNIST ART AND
DESIGN FROM THE FORMER YUGOSLAVIA.

THE BOUNDARIES BETWEEN LIVING SPACE AND GALLERY SPACE
ARE BLURRED: IS THE BICYCLE AN EXHIBIT, OR A MODE OF
TRANSPORT?

A SUMPTUOUS METALLIC BACKDROP INGENIOUSLY LINKED THE MODERN ARCHITECTURE WITH THE ORNATE, HISTORICAL EXHIBITS.

RUSSIAN EVOLUTION

The transformation of the 17th-century Amstelhof into a satellite of the HERMITAGE restored the building's original beauty – while taking it into the 21st century.

WORDS **JANE SZITA**
PHOTOS **ROOS ALDERSHOFF**

Perhaps it's the frothy ball gowns on display at the Hermitage on the Amstel's inaugural exhibition, but the words 'Cinderella-like transformation' keep springing to mind. After all, until recently this building was quite possibly the world's oldest old folks' home, a function it had retained for well over 300 years. Now, however, the stately but sober Amstelhof has been reborn as a serenely appointed satellite of the glittering Hermitage Museum. Old photos on show around the place remind you of the cramped, dingy labyrinth it used to be – in total contrast to its newfound airy elegance.

Although this new Hermitage in Amsterdam could fit into its St Petersburg parent many times over, by Dutch standards it's a palatial building. But there the resemblance to the baroque Russian building ends.

Architecturally, the Amstelhof is an imposing example of Dutch classicism at its most austere: high on symmetry and order, devoid of decoration. But by 2007, when the last elderly resident departed, the building's interior was a sad mishmash of aesthetically challenged alterations. For architect Hans van Heeswijk, called in to renovate the building for its new role, the only solution was to strip the Amstelhof down to its shell.

'Restoring the building to its classical floor plan was the answer to our biggest problem – the conversion of the Amstelhof into a public venue,' says Van Heeswijk. 'The fact is that every day thousands of people visit the museum for the first time, and they need to feel at home quickly if they're going to want to come back.' The building has four wings, arranged around

an expansive main courtyard. Van Heeswijk switched the main entrance to the waterfront side of the building on the Amstel, thus leading visitors across the courtyard and into the lobby. 'The view across the courtyard allows them to see the whole building at a glance, and to understand its scale and how it works,' says the architect. 'And it means the museum faces the city, has a relationship with it.'

Inside the entrance lobby, the whole axis is visible. Clear sightlines entice visitors into the north and south wings, where the main exhibition spaces are. These lofty double-height galleries, measuring 34 by 10 m, were originally open rectangular courtyards flanking the main courtyard of the 17th-century building. They had been filled in with two floors of boxy rooms by later builders, but sweeping these >>>

MERKX+GIROD, THE AMSTERDAM HERMITAGE'S INTERIOR DESIGNERS, CREATED THE OPENING EXHIBITION ON THE RUSSIAN COURT – COMPLETE WITH REVOLVING GLASS CASES FOR THE BALLGOWNS.

THE DOUBLE HEIGHT OF THE TWO MAIN EXHIBITION HALLS CREATES
LONG VIEWS AND INTERESTING PERSPECTIVES.

'We wanted to avoid filling the whole space with function'
HANS VAN HEESWIJK

THE STAIRS WITH A VIEW OF NEVA, THE RESTAURANT,
WITH ITS GLOWING BAR DESIGNED BY MERKX+GIROD.
PHOTO LUUK KRAMER

interventions away revealed the clean lines and harmonious proportions that are now enhanced by curved glass ceilings that drench the galleries in daylight. 'Light is very important in a museum,' says Van Heeswijk. 'People instinctively walk towards it.' His interior uses light to flood the corners of the building, encouraging the flow of traffic throughout the entire space. The staircases – broad, open replacements for the dark, narrow originals – are sited in these light-filled corners, where all three floors are clearly visible; next to them, lift shafts in glass and steel continue the theme of transparency. Materials were used to differentiate between the building as monument and its function as museum. Classical materials – stucco walls, oak flooring, grey pietra serena – are used in what might be called the structure's 'historical fabric', while

glass and steel make the modern interventions – lifts, stairs, reception desk – visually distinct. The interior design, by Merkx+Girod, matches the lyrical simplicity of the original structure.

'It was one of our aims to avoid filling the entire space with function, while creating as much light and space as possible,' explains Van Heeswijk. 'The idea was to separate the modern functions and use them rather like big furniture elements, in order to generate a more spatial quality and to make the structure clearly visible.' This approach allows the building – and its exhibitions – to shine together but separately, rather than privileging one at the expense of the other. Voids, long views through the building and transparent elements lighten and update the Amstelhof's classical formalism. The huge volumes of the main exhibition spaces are

contrasted with the more intimate atmosphere of the small 'cabinet' rooms, each with its own window. All this was achieved on budget (€40 million) and on time, with work taking just two years to complete. 'It was a huge advantage that the museum is run by a private foundation rather than a government body,' says Van Heeswijk. 'It meant we had no red tape to deal with and work could proceed fast.' Funding came in equal parts from national and local government agencies and private sponsors. The City of Amsterdam donated the building. Running costs are covered by sponsorship and ticket sales, with the St Petersburg Hermitage getting €1 of every ticket sold. Cultural entrepreneur Ernst Veen, who initiated and oversaw the project, is now the museum's director. It has to be said that the opening

MERKX+GIROD'S SEEMINGLY HAND-DRAWN METALLIC GRAPHICS ADDED A PLAYFUL TOUCH TO THE FORMAL OBJECTS ON SHOW.

PHOTO LUUK KRAMER

STEEL AND GLASS CREATE LIGHT, AIRY, AND RESOLUTELY MODERN STAIRCASES.
PHOTO LUUK KRAMER

exhibition, devoted to the stuffy Russian court and packing 1800 pieces into the space, does not show off the museum to its best advantage. Windows have been blocked and daylight banished to prevent the costumes on display from fading. But the space still sings. And the next exhibition, Pioneers of Modern Art, devoted to Matisse and designed by Wim Crouwel, promises a better match with the qualities of the interior.

'A museum is a public building. It has to be neutral and abstract, and it has to let the collection or exhibition stand out,' says Hans van Heeswijk. 'Architects invariably think that a museum has to be an ambitious project in which to show off their architectural skills. But I think you need to be modest and aware – and to avoid putting too much of yourself into a building.' ■

PROJECT NAME Hermitage Amsterdam
ARCHITECT Hans van Heeswijk
WEBSITE heeswijk.nl
INTERIOR DESIGN Merkx+Girod
WEBSITE merkx-girod.nl
LANDSCAPE DESIGN Michael van Gessel
LOCATION Amsterdam
CLIENT Stichting Hermitage aan de Amstel
MATERIALS Various
CONSTRUCTION: Bouwbedrijf MJ De Nijs en Zonen, and others
TOTAL FLOOR AREA 9000m²
STAR PIECE depends on exhibition
TYPICAL VISITOR depends on exhibition
NUMBER OF VISITORS PER YEAR Estimated 300.000/year. In 2009, between the opening of 19 June until October 360.000 visitors.
UPCOMING EXHIBITION Pioneers of Modern Art (March 2010)
PERMANENT EXHIBITION The Amstelhof Room and Russia Room are used for permanent exhibitions on the History of Amstelhof, and the history between the St Petersburg Hermitage and Amsterdam Hermitage Museum.
SPECIALISATION Loans from the collection of the Russian State Hermitage Museum in St Petersburg.

MERKX+GIROD FURNISHED THE FUNCTIONAL AREAS, LIKE THE MUSEUM ENTRANCE, TO HIGHLIGHT THE CONTRAST BETWEEN THE BUILDINGS ANCIENT STRUCTURE AND ITS MODERN FUNCTION.
PHOTO LUUK KRAMER

OASIS OF KNOWLEDGE

At San Diego's Fashion Institute of Design and Merchandising, spin doctor CLIVE WILKINSON put contemporary ways of learning centre stage.

WORDS **ALEXANDRA ONDERWATER**
PHOTOS **BENNY CHAN (FOTOWORKS)**

FULL-HEIGHT WALL GRAPHICS OF ABSTRACTED VEGETATION,
FOUND IN THE FIDM STORE AND ELSEWHERE IN THE BUILDING,
REFER TO THE REGION'S DESERT LANDSCAPE.

THE FOCAL POINT OF THE INTERIOR DESIGN IS A GLASS-WALLED LIBRARY.

'Style is just the outside of content'
JEAN-LUC GODARD

A 'PATH' OF SAND-COLOURED QUARTZ-COMPOSITE FLOORING PASSES A LIBRARY, LOUNGES AND FACILITIES SUCH AS FINANCIAL SERVICES.

The formula is crystal clear. You've been commissioned to design a school of higher education, so you do the necessary research. What do students like? What do they need? When Los Angeles-based architect Clive Wilkinson was asked to design the Fashion Institute of Design and Merchandising (FIDM) in San Diego, he went looking for answers to those questions and integrated the results into his design.

Essential to today's educational environment is a good number of inviting communal spaces: informal spots where students can hang out and share information. Studying together facilitates the learning process, a not insignificant fact in an era marked by a surplus of information pouring in from digital media and other modern methods of communication. How to use and filter all this

information is something students pick up from one another on that broad stairway in the hall or on a bench outside. 'Peer-to-peer learning' is the specialist term for information gathered beyond the walls of the classroom.

How do you use architecture to interpret this concept? Stimulating interaction among students requires spacious circulation zones rather than walled cubicles. Areas that up the value of that inevitable scurry from class to class. In terms of spatial composition, today's school demands a broad central 'path' flanked on opposite sides by classrooms, study halls and a library.

And the reception area? Wilkinson doesn't consider reception worthy of a key position, since a school exists, first and foremost, for those students who attend on a regular basis. He would rather make the library a focal point. How?

With a bold lemon yellow, for example – a colour that dominates the desert landscape not far from the school's location. And now that the discussion has shifted to colour, why not use desert hues throughout the rest of the school? Shades of orange, yellow and green – not to mention the blinding blue of the sky.

Characterizing Wilkinson's designs is an aura of childlike simplicity, which is expressed by the architect's use of cartoonish forms, bright colours and a lucid design language. If architects were to make books, Wilkinson's publications would feature an extra-large font. You don't get lost in his interiors or stumble across the kind of inefficient ambiguities that his colleagues sometimes use in an apparent attempt to rival his work. 'Content is the basis of style' greets visitors to the firm's website. Sounds very much

WILKINSON'S INTERIORS FEATURE STRIKING FORMS, BRIGHT COLOURS AND A LUCID DESIGN LANGUAGE, AS EXEMPLIFIED BY THIS COUNTER IN THE LIBRARY.

THE DESERT LANDSCAPE SURROUNDING SAN DIEGO PROVIDED INSPIRATION FOR WILKINSON'S SAND-COLOURED QUARTZ-COMPOSITE FLOORING, OAK-PANELLED CEILING AND COLOUR SCHEME.

like something French film director Jean-Luc Godard once said: 'To me, style is just the outside of content.'

Wilkinson's ability to distil essential elements into a spatial translation that is both literal and abstract leads to legible landscapes with unique personalities. Does the building that houses Disney Store HQ (2007) have brick walls? Then let's make brick the basis of our interventions and give the office interior a Lego-like appearance. In the conference room, for example, we'll install a colourful modular puzzle wall that can be dismantled to form individual seats for meetings. We can also use Honeycomb, a modular display system of stacked hexagonal cells that doubles as a partition, eliminating the need for a permanent wall. Would the staff at ad agency Mother (2004) – an office bursting

its seams – benefit from a more communicative workplace? No problem. Wilkinson simply morphs the existing office table into a mammoth surface of concrete slabs that offers elbow room to 200 people and immediately integrates the staircase into his new scheme.

At Googleplex (2005), the Mountain View headquarters of the successful search engine, Wilkinson applied 'googling' to the configuration of the office space. In recent years he has built a reputation on nomadic workspaces – 'When you're not in your office, you can still be working' (see *Frame* 52, page 161) – in which the concept of a shared environment takes centre stage. His open-plan offices, invariably with lots of glass, allow employees to 'camp' in different rooms. Wilkinson's other showpiece, the urban plan superimposed on the (work)space – complete

with a high street lined by numerous function zones – failed to live up to its promise at Googleplex, however. Strange but true, his '13 ways to collaborate' strategy proved to be too progressive for the young organization.

Fortunately, FIDM gave Wilkinson carte blanche to design the San Diego school. He had already done the interiors of FIDM branches in Orange County (2001) and Los Angeles (2004), and even though the San Diego outpost is seen as their kid brother, Wilkinson says it's the coolest of the three. 'Thanks to our long working relationship [the San Diego school is Wilkinson's 14th project for FIDM], we truly understand what the institution stands for,' he says. 'The whole school is shaped around the students' experience. Staff members, normally treated like superstars, are put in the background. >>>

THE LIBRARY IS VISIBLE IMMEDIATELY UPON ENTERING THE BUILDING.

CLASSROOMS HAVE GLAZED WALLS TO PROMOTE OPENNESS AND INTERACTION. THE RED COMPUTER LOUNGE FORMS A RIGHT ANGLE.

Studying together facilitates the learning process

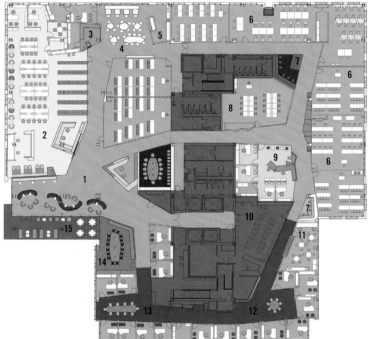

FLOOR PLAN.

1 RECEPTION
2 LIBRARY
3 STORE
4 STUDENT LOUNGE
5 PANTRY
6 CLASSROOM
7 COMPUTER LOUNGE
8 COMPUTER LAB
9 FINANCIAL SERVICES
10 COLLEGE SERVICES
11 EDUCATION AND PLACEMENT
12 FACULTY LOUNGE
13 ADMISSIONS
14 CONFERENCE ROOM
15 TERRACE

Being aware of this approach helps architecturally. We created a little village around the student, with the glass-façade library placed front row – instead of the usual reception counter.'

Those attending FIDM Orange County move through a trendy hot-pink environment, while students at the Los Angeles school live the California dream, complete with palm-fringed pool area. The new San Diego campus, which opened last year, reflects the cultural background of southern California. 'A hundred years ago, there was nothing here,' says Wilkinson. 'The area exemplifies human imposition on nature.' He translated this idea into a palette that captures not only the sparse plant life of the surrounding desert, but also the cultural character of the region: surfers

on slick, shiny boards; seductive signage; and cars. 'Actually, the bright yellow library is done in local car paint.' The explosion of colour on the walls contrasts with the sand-coloured quartz-composite flooring and expansive oak-panelled ceiling. Full-height wall graphics of abstracted vegetation provide visual texture.

Wilkinson's celebrated urban grid appears in this project as well. An open corridor meanders through the space. 'We located elements like a student café, admission desks, career-guidance areas, labs and a student lounge along the path, so it doesn't get too boring.' And the idea behind it? 'Think of it as a piece of music, with a certain rhythm and crescendo moments where the space starts to transform.'

The organic arch of the ceiling in the student lounge features folded strips of galvanized steel,

a reference to the roofs of houses in this part of the city. 'I looked for an inexpensive solution for integrating the air conditioning,' says Wilkinson. 'And this is cheaper than using paper.' Instantly, he comes up with an analogy: 'See, it mimics a ruffled Elizabethan collar.' When I ask if that's something he thought of before or after the ceiling was in place, the imposing South African – all 193 cm of him – has to laugh. 'Design often needs stories to sell itself.'

The client is extremely happy. 'They feel the San Diego campus best reflects their identity now. If you'd envision architecture as clothing, they are now dressed in the right clothes for 2009.' ∎

THE RED COMPUTER LOUNGE STANDS OUT FROM ITS MORE
NEUTRALLY COLOURED SURROUNDINGS LIKE A 'MONUMENT
IN A LANDSCAPE', SAYS WILKINSON.

THAT'S THE SPIRIT

MINISTRY OF DESIGN translated the traditions and symbols associated with advertising giant Leo Burnett into a new office in Singapore.

WORDS **FEMKE DE WILD**
PHOTOS **EDWARD HENDRICKS (CI&A PHOTOGRAPHY)**

GREETING VISITORS IN THE ENTRANCE AREA IS A 3-M-HIGH, GRAFFITI-LIKE PORTRAIT OF LEO BURNETT, 'THE MAN BEHIND THE BRAND'. IN HIS HAND IS THE ICONIC BLACK PENCIL ASSOCIATED WITH THE COMPANY.

MINISTRY OF DESIGN HEAPED
ALL THE AGENCY'S PRIZE-WINNING
TROPHIES INTO A WHEELBARROW
AND ILLUMINATED THEM
WITH A SPOTLIGHT.

SCREENS INTEGRATED INTO THE WHITE COUNTER DISPLAY
VIDEOS MADE BY THE AD AGENCY. SOUND EMANATES
FROM HANGING 'DOMES'.

EVERY LEO BURNETT OFFICE RESERVES
A PLACE FOR RED APPLES.

'Any good space is about how it benefits the user'
COLIN SEAH

'We wanted Leo Burnett to be present in the office, overlooking everything like a ghost.' Speaking is Colin Seah of Ministry of Design, the firm behind new offices in Singapore for ad agency Leo Burnett. Even today, the point of departure for the design of these interiors emerged from traditions that the spiritual father of many world-famous ad campaigns developed during the early years of his company.

After establishing his firm in 1935, Leo Burnett quickly became one of the most influential people in the world of advertising. He believed in the power of visual symbols and was able to reach the consumer on a subconscious level with icons like the Marlboro Man and Tony the Tiger, who still appears on Kellogg's cereal boxes. For his own office, Burnett came up with two symbols that are still part of the corporate identity:

a red apple and a big black pencil. Above all else, Seah's client wanted these symbols to be part of the new interior.

Visitors to the agency's website find an animation in which the illustrious pencil draws a portrait of Burnett. To impress visitors entering the office in Singapore, Seah installed a similar graffiti-like portrait in the lobby, but this one is three metres high. He brought in an artist to apply the work to floor and walls. 'It had to look as though the portrait was drawn by an invisible hand,' says Seah. 'The lines had to radiate movement, be informal *and* creative, and show that Burnett's soul is still at the heart of the company.'

As you exit the lift and turn left, you enter the reception area, which is dominated by a long, white counter. Hanging above the counter is

a transparent bowl filled with fresh red apples. 'The company was founded during the Great Depression. While everybody else cut expenses, Burnett started giving apples to clients and employees,' says Seah. 'The story goes that the receptionist put them behind locked doors every single day before she went home. They represented honesty, integrity and simplicity. That thought is very relevant these days.' On small screens in the counter, you can watch advertising films made by the firm. Sound emanates from semicircular speakers suspended like pendant lamps above the screens. 'Ad agencies usually show off with loud ads and huge billboards. We opted for a more intimate and subtle approach; these domes keep the sound focused.' A large white projection screen on a wall beyond the counter looks >>>

PLYWOOD DESKS IN THE OPEN-PLAN OFFICE HAVE BEEN PAINTED IN VARIOUS COLOURS TO CREATE A CHEQUERBOARD PATTERN.

like those used in cinemas. 'We wanted not only to show modern, high-tech films but also to refer to traditional resources used in the early years of the company,' he continues. A conspicuous spotlight dramatically illuminates a wheelbarrow standing in front of the screen; it's heaped to the brim with the highly prestigious prizes awarded to Burnett ad campaigns over the years. 'They were in ugly display cases at the old office. This is more blasé. Here and there we were a bit cheeky.'

Another cheeky element can be seen on the outside of the building. 'Ads are judged on a scale of one to ten. One is the worst piece of advertising, and anything from seven on up is really good. Leo Burnett wants all its campaigns to score a seven or higher. That's why 7+ is the third symbol that has been integrated into every Burnett office building worldwide,' explains Seah,

who translated that goal into a work of art on the façade. When viewed from close by, it looks like nothing more than several long black lines; when you look at it from the right perspective, however, you clearly see a 7+. 'Ad people often *talk* a lot more than they *do*. We wanted to point out the difficulty in achieving a 7+. It's our way of teasing them.'

The old Singapore office had been a hive of small rooms – individual cubicles for each member of the staff. With a more cooperative, open workplace in mind, Seah created a large uninterrupted space in which everyone sits at long wooden desks. 'Being on a limited budget, we didn't have money for an expensive, wear-resistant, white finish.' Making a virtue of necessity, he had plywood painted in various colours to form a pattern. 'These offices contrast

with the building's shiny white public spaces; the pattern is the feature here.

'People are always reluctant to change,' he remarks. 'Everybody was used to having his or her own little kingdom, which is not part of the new design. We suggested making a wall in which each of them has a special spot.' Every employee was given an apple to 'customize'. All the apples are displayed in a wall of small cabinets in the lunch area. 'Details like that are important. The agency is nothing without its employees.'

Seah also incorporated a well-known Leo Burnett saying into the interior. 'The founder was always talking about reaching for the stars and the constellations,' he says. 'Various drawings show him literally reaching for the stars, so we made a corridor of stars.' >>>

LONG LINES ON PATIO AND FAÇADE FORM A 7+ WHEN VIEWED FROM A DISTANCE; 7+ IS THE AGENCY'S BENCHMARK NUMBER WITH REGARD TO THE SUCCESS OF AN AD CAMPAIGN.

COMMENTING ON THE MEETING ROOMS, COLIN SEAH CALLS THEM 'THE ONLY SPACE IN THE OFFICE THAT HAS NO NATURAL LIGHT, AND THAT'S SOMETHING I WANTED TO DRAMATIZE'.

'I perceive interior design and architecture as a continuity of ideas'

COLIN SEAH

A DIM CORRIDOR PUNCTUATED WITH GREEN OPENINGS REFERS TO BURNETT'S MOTTO – 'REACH FOR THE STARS AND THE CONSTELLATIONS' – AND LEADS TO MEETING ROOMS.

A dark passageway leads to the heart of the office, where meeting rooms are located. Round openings in the walls of the corridor light up like stars in the night sky and, at the same time, offer a view of what's happening inside these rooms, which are immersed entirely in green, the corporate colour. 'It's the only space in the office that has no natural light. I wanted to dramatize this and to create a theatrical experience for people entering here.'

In its campaigns, Leo Burnett takes what the company calls the 'HumanKind approach', which is marked by a focus on human behaviour that's much more than simply conveying a brand message. Seah, too, gives user experience a front-row seat. 'Any good space is about how it benefits the user,' he says. 'It's about humankind. It's bigger than any concept.'

Seah applies this theory not only to interiors but also to architecture commissions, which have been claiming an increasing amount of his time and effort. 'What I learned from The Great Indoors Awards that Frame organized for the first time two years ago [see *Frame* 60, page 145] is that the best results are achieved when the designer has control of both interior design and architecture. Since then, I've focused more and more on a holistic approach. I'm not interested in blurring the boundaries between disciplines, but in perceiving all elements as a continuity of ideas. There lies the future.' ∎

ACCENTS IN 'CORPORATE GREEN' ADD VITALITY TO THE PREDOMINANTLY WHITE LUNCH AND MEETING AREAS.

AN 'APPLE WALL' IN SINGAPORE FEATURES CUSTOMIZED APPLES MADE BY EMPLOYEES.

Walk *the* LINE

THE ENTRANCE, AS SEEN FROM THE EAST.

The simple, concrete house that BOYD CODY built in rural Ireland is designed to be filled with sunlight, weather permitting.

WORDS **CHARLOTTE VAUDREY**
PHOTOS **PAUL TIERNEY**

THE LIVING ROOM, AS SEEN FROM THE SOUTHWEST.

Ireland's daily dose of sunshine drops from an average of five and a half hours a day in June to one hour a day in December, according to the Irish Meteorological Service. Peter Cody, the joint founder of the Dublin-based firm Boyd Cody Architects, is more keenly aware than most of what the country is missing, having enjoyed several years of work in sunnier climes. Although it's over a decade since Cody returned to Ireland to establish his practice, the desire to make the most of the sunlight, should there happen to be any, can be seen in the firm's signature supersize windows and glazed walls.

When the opportunity arose for Boyd Cody Architects to design a house for Cody himself in the village where he grew up, channelling sunlight into the building was, naturally, a key factor. Cody envisaged the single-floor

Bohermore House as a row of volumes equal in width but gradually increasing in depth. Assigning a single function to each, he based these allocations on the amount of space required: the entrance needed the least and the sitting room the most. Cody then pulled the five volumes apart, creating a spine-like configuration connected by a central corridor. Voids separating the various volumes became open-ended courtyards looking out on surrounding fields and hills. Peter Cody explains: 'The courtyards mediate between the internal rooms and the broader landscape.'

Because mere windows wouldn't bring in sufficient light, Cody glazed the long sides of each volume (with the obvious exception of bathroom and entry) from floor to ceiling. The effect is astonishing.

At night, the glazing is all but invisible, transforming the uncluttered volumes into what looks like an open, Mediterranean villa. By day, with a row of majestic trees framing one side of the house, a mountain range in the distance and every available sunbeam making a difference to the level of natural light inside, the house showcases central Ireland at its best.

In addition, rather than orientating the house directly southwards, Cody positioned it so that the angle of each glazed wall maximizes the amount of sunlight spilling into the east-facing bedroom, the sitting room to the south and the dining room and kitchen to the west. Massive, floor-to-ceiling, sliding timber doors in every glazed wall open both sides of each volume to the courtyards, almost doubling the existing 100 m² of habitable space. >>>

THE DINING ROOM, WITH GLAZED WALLS FACING NORTHEAST AND SOUTHWEST.

'To look across Bohermore diagonally, is to experience it as part of the landscape'
PETER CODY

BEDROOM AND KITCHEN, AS
SEEN FROM THE DINING ROOM.

Views through the house from one volume across a courtyard to another have been carefully managed. The short wall of each volume is solid concrete; in each case the deliberately framed view from inside allows occupants to see only one other area, avoiding what would otherwise be a jumble of overlapping spaces. Each room is furnished very sparsely to ensure that the view into another volume is serene rather than hectic; in so doing, Cody achieved a harmonious feeling comparable to the ambience that Jun Igarashi created in House O in northern Japan. Although the rural location of Bohermore House enabled Boyd Cody to use transparency in an almost unprecedented way for a ground-floor-only dwelling – quite unlike House O's urgent need for privacy – the two projects have many aspects in common.

'To look across Bohermore diagonally, from room to courtyard to the field beyond, is to experience it as part of the landscape,' says Cody. He enhanced the blurring of the boundary between indoors and out by having certain internal walls mirror external surfaces. He also extended the polished concrete floor into two courtyards. Inside, a single step down between parallel volumes subtly articulates their status as independent spaces. The gentle drop in level aligns the floor with the same gradient as the meadow it sits in. Meanwhile, growing overhead on the flat roof is a 'sebum blanket which replaces the building's footprint'. Looking at the house from outside, you note that the industrial aesthetic of the angular, concrete volumes is quite brutal, contrasting sharply with Cody's intention for the house to blend seamlessly

with the landscape. Intriguingly, although the surrounding landscape is beautiful, none of the furniture is arranged so that people can take in the scenic outdoor vistas. The galley kitchen is the most extreme example. For practicality, its units face the plumbing wall shared with the bathroom. The unfortunate result is a cook forced to ignore the view while preparing a snack or meal. Although Jun Igarashi's House O has an internal focus as well, the architect's reasoning is more transparent: because neighbouring buildings are so tall, Igarashi stretched each volume of the house metres higher, allowing his elevated windows to draw light into the residence without jeopardizing the privacy of the occupants. The proportions of each volume in Cody's original concept have a measured logic. But the rhythm is interrupted

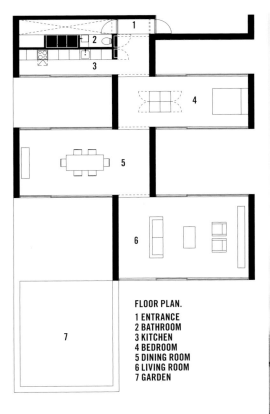

FLOOR PLAN.
1 ENTRANCE
2 BATHROOM
3 KITCHEN
4 BEDROOM
5 DINING ROOM
6 LIVING ROOM
7 GARDEN

WALLS ARE MADE OF LOAD-BEARING, CONCRETE BLOCKS.

THE KITCHEN IS PART OF THE BATHROOM-AND-ENTRANCE BLOCK.

DIAGRAM SHOWING
THE PROGRESSION IN ROOM
SIZES IN THE HOUSE.

in the kitchen and bathroom block, which – instead of being a door's width plus a metre, as the concept dictated (he added 1 m to each successive volume) – has been expanded until it almost merges with the entry. The view through the house was not affected, though; it's only the bird's-eye view of the building that's lost its impact.

Cody's floor plan is dictated by the size of each volume rather than by overlapping functions of the spaces contained. The resulting layout is unusual, with the bedroom separating the kitchen and dining room, and the kitchen between bedroom and bathroom. Just as Jun Igarashi did in designing House O, Cody reworked the framework of the floor plan, ignoring the hierarchy of room allocation to come up with a more inventive alternative.

Reflecting another similarity to Igarashi's project in Japan, Bohermore's unconventional design has implications for utility bills. To offset these costs, Igarashi used insulated concrete that retains heat, and Boyd Cody installed an environmentally friendly heat pump to power underfloor heating.

When the property bubble burst in 2008, Ireland's economy was as badly hit as that of many other countries. Whether or not Bohermore was seen as a handy filler for a gap in commissions, the decision to go ahead with the project has proved a sound one. In addition to gathering local accolades, Bohermore House has been short-listed for the 2009 World Architecture Festival Awards. ∎

Let it ROLL

A house in Japan by JUN IGARASHI has sound reasons for its seemingly chaotic configuration.

WORDS **CHARLOTTE VAUDREY**
PHOTOS **SERGIO PIRRONE**

Picture a cityscape that is almost unique in Japan. A cluster of buildings, ranging in height from 2.5 to 6 m, looks like a collection of smartly finished shipping containers. No fewer than 15 volumes in total, they are actually interconnected and form the residence of a young Japanese couple. An outstretched, single-floor dwelling on a generous piece of land is almost unheard of in Japan. For the couple in question, living in an area that is suffering industrial decline and out-migration has an up side: the corresponding affordability of relatively large building sites. Factor in the location – Rubeshibe, a small town in a remote area of Hokkaido, a province in northern Japan – and the image becomes clearer still.

Although House O, by Jun Igarashi Architects, has a completely different layout from

Bohermore House, the residential project that Boyd Cody realized in rural Ireland, the two have a surprising number of elements in common. Both comprise a series of volumes of differing sizes and are one-floor residences conceived to make the best of a specific climate. Although neither is large (at just over 112 m², House O is a shade bigger than Boyd Cody's 100-m² project), each has such an unusual layout that, judged on outward appearances alone, the overall impression is one of multiple dwellings.

The bird's-eye view of House O is extraordinary. The footprint of the residence looks as if it was created by drawing around the outlines of a jumble of big boxes dropped from the sky. Although the configuration seems chaotic, especially when compared with Boyd Cody's linear Bohermore House, the logic behind

Igarashi's programme is just as considered. Igarashi's studio abandoned initial plans for a squared-off, rational layout, because fitting in all functions requested by the client necessitated extra circulation areas and what the architect calls 'rooms and views orientated in an irrational manner'. The solution was to make a paper cutout of every single space in the programme and to position each one in 'the most favourable location and orientation'.

The main window in the kitchen, for example, faces the orchard and garden to the south. Once the location of the kitchen had been established, Igarashi connected the dining room to it, and so on. 'We got rid of the hierarchy that normally determines where you locate a room,' he says. 'From certain points on the site, the house may look symmetrical, but if you take one step >>>

A VIEW THAT INCLUDES BOTH WASHING ROOM AND BEDROOM.

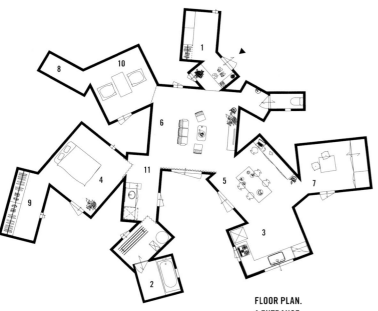

FLOOR PLAN.
1 ENTRANCE
2 BATHROOM
3 KITCHEN
4 BEDROOM
5 DINING ROOM
6 LIVING ROOM
7 JAPANESE ROOM
8 STORAGE ROOM
9 WALK-IN CLOSET
10 GUEST ROOM
11 WASHING ROOM

THE CENTRALLY LOCATED LIVING ROOM.

THE DINING ROOM, NEXT TO THE KITCHEN.

RENDERINGS OF
HOUSE O FROM THREE
PERSPECTIVES.

in either direction, the form changes. It's similar to phenomena seen in nature.'

Like Boyd Cody, Jun Igarashi was strongly influenced by climate; but unlike the stable if unexceptional weather around Bohermore, the extremes in temperature experienced by buildings in Hokkaido presented the Japanese team with additional challenges. House O had to be comfortable during Rubeshibe's hot summers and bitterly cold winters. The plan the studio devised creates 'nooks and crannies' all around the exterior, which are either lit by the sun or sheltered by shade. Windows are positioned to take advantage of the orientation of the wall in question. Few windows face directly south – a deliberate choice made to avoid the excessive heat of summer – but most occupy walls on the south side of the house, where exterior niches

shield windows from the worst of the winter winds and snow. 'The form was inspired by a certain kind of desert cactus,' says Igarashi in explaining House O. 'A cross section shows it has folds on its surface that create shade to keep it cool. Drawing from a simple, natural phenomenon, we found a starting point for a new type of architecture.'

Although the building density in this area is low, and the couple's neighbours are not especially close, privacy was nonetheless an issue because buildings closest to the house – a hospital and a factory – are tall. Igarashi solved the problem with excessively high walls featuring elevated windows that allow light to enter the house but do nothing to disturb the desired privacy. Igarashi also played with ceiling heights.

By making the ceiling in each volume a different height, he established a refreshing atmosphere throughout the dwelling, thus answering the couple's request for something that would distract them from the lack of variation in floor levels – far too monotonous for their liking. The centrally positioned living room is the loftiest space, at an eye-popping 6 m. From the living room, the volumes drop in height according to function and location. Ceilings in the dining room and bedroom are still a staggering 5 m high, however, and those in both guest room and kitchen could accommodate, if need be, a 4-m-high giant. The soaring environment within House O is on a par with the transparency of Bohermore House, as the impact of both is a cleverly created sense of spaciousness. ■

THE GREAT INDOORS AWARD 2009 CELEBRATING THE BEST INTERIORS WORLDWIDE *changing ideals*

AND THE WINNER IS

NO CHANGING IDEALS

The second edition of **THE GREAT INDOORS AWARD** yielded an embarrassment of riches, but few projects reflecting societal change.

WORDS **GUUS BEUMER**

FROM LEFT: JOEP VAN LIESHOUT, ANNIINA KOIVU, ANNE HØJGAARD JØRGENSEN, LINDE DORENBOSCH, GUUS BEUMER, DIRK VAN DEN HEUVEL, GIULIO RIDOLFO AND JO COENEN.

Surely there's no better time to analyse developments within the field of interior design than during an international competition. Can we spot trends that say something about the direction the discipline is taking? About its relationship to the times? Its role in society? A major objective of The Great Indoors Award, a competition introduced in 2007, is to address and, if possible, answer these questions.

The initiators of the first edition of The Great Indoors asked entrants to look at the interior as our last utopia, a utopia that proceeded to make its mark on public space as well. For the second edition of the competition, held in the autumn of 2009, the organizers chose the theme 'Changing Ideals', which they based on an exhibition of the same name mounted by NaiM/Bureau Europa. Underlying both the exhibition and the competition is the belief that changing social ideals have direct consequences for interior design. The competition organizers were convinced that the current economic crisis would have an impact on the jury's perspective – an impact that would also affect projects realized before the crisis had struck its first perceptible blow.

On 23 October at nine in the morning, an international jury convened in Maastricht to select five nominees for each of the categories and, eventually, five winners. The jury faced a daunting task: more than 380 entrants from 40 countries had submitted projects to The Great Indoors Award 2009. Members of the jury were motivated, however, by the wide range of talent represented among the entries and by the opportunity to survey work by both internationally acclaimed designers and relatively unknown names.

LOOKING FOR LEITMOTIFS

After a brief examination of all entries, jury members set out to discover whether a closer analysis would reveal one or more easily recognizable leitmotifs, but they soon saw the impossibility of formulating a pervasive motivating force. Although basic principles appeared in a number of individual projects – concerns such as sustainability, recycling, impermanence and the desire for a public space – an all-encompassing train of thought was difficult to identify. And any such attempt would show little regard for the diversity of the entries.

The impossibility of finding any sort of obvious theme running through the submitted projects came as somewhat of a surprise. More than once, members of the jury were heard speculating on what they might have missed. Had they failed to detect an overriding truth in the aspect of clientship, of functionality, of budgets – something that had managed to conceal the more external or more social considerations? Finally, after even deeper scrutiny of the projects and categories involved in the competition, the jury again came to the conclusion that – although the organizers' desire to link the theme of 'Changing Ideals' to the material submitted by the contestants was an understandable goal – the only answer lay in the individual qualities of each project.

FURTHER REFLECTION

Despite the absence of a leitmotif, was it possible to offer general comments of any kind at all? The jury was impressed, even more than its predecessor had been in 2007, by the level of

quality that marked these projects. The number of entries that had to be set aside for failing to satisfy the minimum requirements was negligible. Whether submitted by an unknown designer from a new economy or a famous creative from an established centre of design, virtually every project represented a position of interest to the jury and a position that warranted full comparative assessment.

A discussion with an explicitly fundamental character – and one that transcended the diversity marking these projects – revolved around the distinction between architecture and interior architecture. Whereas certain jury members looked at each entry as an integrated architecture project – an entity comprising skin, skeleton and interior – others focused specifically on the work of the interior architect, claiming that the awards should emphasize this particular aspect of the projects. Putting aside their differences, they decided to approach this matter, too, as it pertained to the individual project.

Although the jury was not interested by definition in the visual language of a project, a great deal of time went into an analysis of the spatial quality underlying the overall image presented by each entry. The most complex matter proved to be the specific cultural context that led to the creation of a project. In most cases, the jury had only the participant's written explanation of the background of a given project. In situations where a specific cultural context could be distilled from the data available and could be used for comparative assessment, the jury considered this information in its evaluation. >>>

FROM LEFT: ANNE HØJGAARD JØRGENSEN, GUUS BEUMER, DIRK VAN DEN HEUVEL AND ROBERT THIEMANN.

THE AWARD

The Great Indoors is an international, biennial, interior-design award. The total amount of prize money is €30,000. The Great Indoors Award honours projects in five categories. The winner of each category receives a monetary prize. In addition to these awards, the event includes workshops led by international design students. Initiators of the award programme are Marres Centre for Contemporary Culture, NaiM/Bureau Europa and Frame Publishers. Sponsors are the province of Limburg and the municipality of Maastricht.

THE JURY

ANNE HØJGAARD JØRGENSEN
Head of design, Kvadrat (DK)
ANNIINA KOIVU
Design editor, *Abitare* magazine (IT)
JOEP VAN LIESHOUT
Artist (NL)
GIULIO RIDOLFO
Colour consultant (IT)
DIRK VAN DEN HEUVEL
Theorist, TU Delft (NL)
JO COENEN
Architect (NL)
GUUS BEUMER (FACILITATING CHAIRMAN)
Director, Marres Centre for Contemporary Culture and NaiM/Bureau Europa (NL)
ROBERT THIEMANN (FACILITATING CHAIRMAN)
Editor in chief, *Frame* magazine (NL)

THE WINNERS

Of the four categories accompanying the Design Firm of the Year award, Show & Sell and Relax & Consume clearly represent the commercial reality of architecture, as well as those concerns inextricably tied to commerce, such as identity, branding and luxury. In the category Show & Sell, OMA's project for Prada is the ineluctable winner. Not one function, but multiple functions; not one atmosphere, but multiple atmospheres; not one perspective, but multiple perspectives. All contained not within a virtual reality but within the project's own materiality: the requirements for realizing this constructivist vision (nearly a century after the heyday of that style) included even hydraulic cranes. The jury considers OMA's project for Prada a perfect example of a project that transcends a commercial reality and injects this with social ambitions, while simultaneously representing both past and future.

The winner in the Relax & Consume category is a noodle restaurant in Las Vegas created by Design Spirits. In this entry, the jury spotted a fresh air of self-awareness: long an importer of design talent, Asia is now exporting creativity – even to locations like Las Vegas, a renowned hub of entertainment. This restaurant design is entertainment, and more than one jury member was entranced by the stratified spectacle of food and design. A play of contrasts blurs any immediate readability of the design and gives the interior more than a mystic quality. The combination of self-awareness, entertainment and stratification makes Beijing Noodle No. 9 an absolute winner.

The categories Concentrate & Collaborate and Serve & Facilitate, on the other hand, are tied to public issues and their underlying social ambitions. An extension of this notion assumes the form of participation, collectivism and the like. In the Concentrate & Collaborate category, an office for a design agency – the work of i29 – captures first prize. Every interior is subject to change and impermanence, but this design unites the temporary and the sustainable. What's more, the designers have not resorted to the aesthetic of impermanence that the jury ascertained in many of the projects examined. Transience is not an ideology here. In this project, the jury finds a pleasing balance of modest means, expressive imagery and effective intervention within an interior that lends shape to society's demand for sustainability in both an aesthetic and a convincing manner.

First prize in the Serve & Facilitate category goes to a temporary university library designed by Ira Koers and Roelof Mulder. The tight budget and the provisional character, in combination with the abstract quality of the design, make this project an impressive winner. Projects completed in recent years – certainly those of a temporary nature – have often been subject to far-reaching thematization. The jury expresses its unanimous appreciation for a design that gives abstract functionality centre stage, while offering room for reflection.

Finally, the jury deliberately chose not to regard the Interior Design Firm of the Year as an oeuvre award but to nominate entries submitted by younger design offices, whose work – in the eyes of the jury – throws a new light on interior design. The winner, Swedish firm Guise, belongs to a genre of younger outfits whose projects combine modest budgets with a highly distinctive approach to interior design. Persuaded by Guise's lucid design methodology and the graphic quality of the work, the jury sees in the firm's pared-down view of design a 'light-touch' scenario for the future, in which simple ingredients can lead to work that effectively communicates a client's identity while also offering maximum functionality. ▬

JOEP VAN LIESHOUT AND ANNIINA KOIVU.

Firm of the Year 2009

MARCH STUDIO

In the two years of its existence, March Studio has made quite a name for itself, thanks to several high-profile projects. March Studio merges a sense of theatricality with ingenious styling and enriches interior architecture by approaching the interior as if it were a stage set: here today, gone tomorrow.
marchstudio.com.au

STUDIO MAKKINK & BEY

Studio Makkink & Bey knows how to marry product design with architecture in a non-hierarchical way. An architectural scale model becomes an end product, for example, as seen at the Droog Design store in New York. The studio's wealth of resources includes reuse, craftsmanship and coauthorship.
jurgenbey.nl

GUISE

Guise combines modest budgets with a highly distinctive approach to interior design. Persuaded by Guise's lucid design methodology and the graphic quality of the work, the jury sees in the firm's pared-down view of design a scenario for the future, in which simple ingredients can lead to work that effectively communicates a client's identity while also offering maximum functionality.
guise.se

I29 INTERIOR ARCHITECTS

Three nominations in one year commandingly illustrate the convincing quality of projects designed and realized by i29 Interior Architects. This firm manages to unite architectural elements and an intensive exploration of surfaces, using colour and/or typography to imbue these surfaces with an extraordinary power of expression.
i29.nl

MAURICE MENTJENS

Handling texture and colour in an inventive way, Maurice Mentjens cleverly lends shape to topical issues. Mentjens can evoke a total scenario with the use of only a few image-determining interventions. His 'light touch' methodology is an innovative response to the extreme makeovers seen in recent years.
mauricementjens.com

Show & Sell

PRADA TRANSFORMER

OFFICE: OMA
CLIENT: PRADA

The ineluctable winner of the Show & Sell category is Prada Transformer. Not one function, but multiple functions; not one atmosphere, but multiple atmospheres; not one perspective, but multiple perspectives. The perfect example of a project that transcends the commercial reality of representation, while simultaneously representing both past and future.
oma.eu

PHOTO UWE WALTER

LEVEL GREEN

OFFICE: J. MAYER H. ARCHITECTS
CLIENT: AUTOSTADT, WOLFSBURG

Here the designers used a recycling logo as a point of departure for an architectural model that is transformed, over and over: each new transformation provides support for an integrated system that seamlessly contains all technological requirements. Model, support function and content are encompassed in one system that generates a layered experience.
jmayerh.de

TECHTILE 2007

OFFICE: NOSIGNER
CLIENT: VIRTUAL REALITY SOCIETY OF JAPAN

This exhibition design consists of nothing but cling film, a material used to cover the floor and to create translucent partitions throughout the space. The project shows that a very limited budget can produce an extraordinary experience and that a material used in a different context can evoke brand-new connotations.
nosigner.com

DJS

OFFICE: PANORAMA
CLIENT: CHINA RESOURCES RETAIL (GROUP) CO.

The ultimate enlargement – a description that applies mainly to the level of materialization achieved by this project – proved irresistibly appealing to the jury. It's the combination of materials and implacable perfection, however, that led to a royal retail experience for a brand that operates, interestingly enough, in the mid-range sector.
panoramahk.com

FIFTH AVENUE SHOE REPAIR

OFFICE: GUISE
CLIENT: FIFTH AVENUE SHOE REPAIR

The keen, clean graphic delineation that highlights this interior fuses with the use of expressive silhouettes to evoke a well-considered, finely nuanced image. The jury praises the crystalline design and sees in this interior a shift in the 'total transformation' concept towards the application of a limited number of sculptural resources.
guise.se

Relax & Consume

HOTEL ZENDEN

OFFICE: WIEL ARETS ARCHITECTS
CLIENT: ZENDEN

The minimalist mastery that went into this hotel and martial-arts academy demanded keen consideration of each decision leading to its realization. It is a space that demonstrates the aphorism 'God is in the details'. Although the project is a renovation, Wiel Arets has used every resource available to meld the sculptural quality of the new interior with its historical context.

wielaretsarchitects.nl

MIRAGE

OFFICE: KJELLGREN KAMINSKY ARCHITECTURE AB
CLIENT: MUNICIPALITY OF VELLINGE

This attempt to integrate location, history and the future features sharply defined walls, both inside and out. Without becoming a stylistic quotation of postmodernism, Mirage recaptures the 1950s through its critical analysis of the modernist tradition.

kjellgrenkaminsky.se

BERGE

OFFICE: NILS HOLGER MOORMANN
CLIENT: NILS HOLGER MOORMANN

Berge is an interior that illustrates one designer's fervent desire to produce work based on tradition. The craftsmanship, references to location and austere artisanal ambience of the interior individually reflect Nils Holger Moormann's intentions. Berge is a protest against the use of a strictly global language in today's interiors.

moormann.de

WINNER

BEIJING NOODLE NO. 9

OFFICE: DESIGN SPIRITS
CLIENT: BEIJING NOODLE

Long an importer of design talent, Asia is now exporting creativity – even to locations like Las Vegas. A play of contrasts blurs any immediate readability of the design and gives the interior more than a mystic quality. The project successfully combines self-awareness, entertainment and stratification.

design-spirits.com

MONDRIAN SOUTH BEACH

OFFICE: MARCEL WANDERS STUDIO
CLIENT: MORGANS HOTEL GROUP

Labelling this project both unique and inevitable is no exaggeration. Here we see a designer at his peak, a man who scores the kind of big-budget commissions that allow him to realize virtually any idea imaginable to inimitable perfection. For this project, Wanders mixed corporate identity and branding with Hollywood glamour and extraordinary theatricality.

marcelwanders.com

Concentrate & Collaborate

SAXO BANK
OFFICE: 3XN
CLIENT: SAXO BANK

A sequel to the classic approach to the office interior is this project by 3xN, an outfit that sees the office as a boundless space featuring fluid transitions. Saxo Bank not only conveys an image of transparency to those outside the building but also, thanks to its interior, gives tangible form to the notion of a close-knit community.
3xn.dk

GUMMO OFFICE
OFFICE: I29 INTERIOR ARCHITECTS
CLIENT: GUMMO

Here the jury recognizes a link between transience and sustainability in a project that does not resort to an aesthetic of impermanence. The design lends shape to society's demand for sustainability in both an aesthetic and a convincing manner. Holding all components of this simple intervention together are the colour black and a lucid zoning plan.
i29.nl

PHOTO COURTESY OF GERMAN TV STATION DEUTSCHE WELLE

THE WHY FACTORY TRIBUNE
OFFICE: MVRDV AND RICHARD HUTTEN
CLIENT: DELFT UNIVERSITY OF TECHNOLOGY

One part of the complex renovation required after a fire at Delft University of Technology was the addition of a multifunctional structure to the inner courtyard of an existing building. The effectiveness of this intervention, which lends new definition to an intermediate space, is worthy of recognition.
mvrdv.nl, richardhutten.com

PHOTO JOACHIM BAAN

FACEBOOK HQ
OFFICE: STUDIO O+A
CLIENT: FACEBOOK

Facebook wanted its head office to project the organization's sense of community. Armed with input from Facebook employees, Studio o+a created an interior that satisfies the brief in an exemplary manner. The preservation of existing architectural details, along with the results of research into energy-efficient lighting and recycled materials, reflects the socially conscious approach of both designers and client.
o-plus-a.com

CARDBOARD-OFFICE-INTERIOR
OFFICE: ALRIK KOUDENBURG (A+ DESIGN DIRECTOR) AND JOOST VAN BLEISWIJK
CLIENT: NOTHING

The quality of this entry – a new hybrid of interior and product design – lies in a fusion of its parts. The jury admires both the choice of material and the methodology on which it is based. The entire office interior is made from cardboard; the components were assembled without the use of screws or adhesives.
alrik.nl, projectjoost.com

Serve & Facilitate

BOOKBUS
OFFICE: MUUNGANO
CLIENT: KIRUNA CITY LIBRARY

Influenced not only by formal and aesthetic criteria but also by social concerns, the interior of the Kiruna City Library represents a modest yet significant contribution to the notion of community and the dissemination of culture. This simple yet effective design provides the perfect vehicle for achieving the client's objectives.
muungano.com

NATIONAL TECHNICAL LIBRARY OF PRAGUE
OFFICE: PROJEKTIL + HIPPOS + PAS + LABORATORY
CLIENT: CZECH MINISTRY OF EDUCATION

The point of this project is not the willingness to approach a public space as a multifunctional venue, but the use of a substantial budget to achieve a specific solution. The key to the success of the design lies in its nuanced spatial development and in the use of colours, materials, unique furniture designs and graphics to define location.
projektil.cz, hipposdesign.com, particip.tv and laboratory.cz

UNIVERSITY OF AMSTERDAM LIBRARY
OFFICE: BUREAU IRA KOERS AND STUDIO ROELOF MULDER
CLIENT: UNIVERSITY OF AMSTERDAM (UVA)

Working on a tight budget, the winner in this category linked the provisional character of the space to an abstract design. The jury expresses its unanimous appreciation for an interior that gives functionality centre stage, while offering room for reflection. This library transcends strictly utilitarian concerns, uniting a contemplative design with academic criteria such as the transfer of knowledge.
irakoers.nl, roelofmulder.nl

POETRY IN MOTION
OFFICE: I29 INTERIOR ARCHITECTS IN COLLABORATION WITH SNELDER ARCHITECTEN
CLIENT: PANTA RHEI COLLEGE

The interior interventions that mark this project exude an air of specificity, which is conveyed both in unique furniture designs and in the architects' concern for the educative task of a school. Every aspect of the interior design expresses a clear visual language. With an exceptionally mature hand, i29 has articulated the various spaces in a highly controlled manner.
i29.nl, snelder.com

ENTRANCE
OFFICE: HAUNTING DOGS FULL OF GRACE
CLIENT: BOIJMANS VAN BEUNINGEN MUSEUM ROTTERDAM

The jury admires the specificity that each of the six designers involved in this project injected into his or her contribution to the entrance area. Of particular interest to the jury is the way in which the designers embraced an intermediate space, using both product design and interior design to create a fluently scaled interior.
wiekisomers.com, bertjanpot.nl
frankbruggeman.com, simonheijdens.com
tednoten.com, jurgenbey.nl

'The deeper you delve into contemporary art,
the more addictive it becomes'
ANDERS BYRIEL, KVADRAT

Angle poise

Nissan's multi-faceted Cube car proves it can cut it as it squares up to the edgiest contemporary architecture

PHOTOGRAPHY: GRÉGOIRE ALEXANDRE WRITER: JONATHAN BELL
SET BUILDER: JEAN-MICHEL BERTIN
PRODUCED BY WALLPAPER* MAGAZINE / BESPOKE

SOFT TOUCH

Driven by a quest for space and tempered by an artistic touch, the Cube's edgy curves offer the same aesthetic thrill as Jakob + MacFarlane's writhing, curvaceous Docks de Paris. The new green construction grows organically out of the original warehouse, thus reinventing the industrial structure

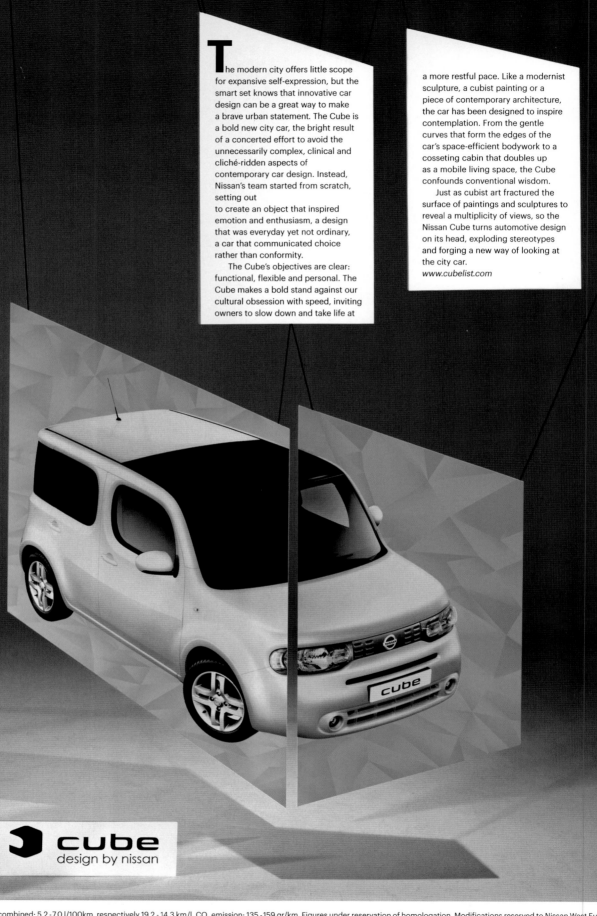

The modern city offers little scope for expansive self-expression, but the smart set knows that innovative car design can be a great way to make a brave urban statement. The Cube is a bold new city car, the bright result of a concerted effort to avoid the unnecessarily complex, clinical and cliché-ridden aspects of contemporary car design. Instead, Nissan's team started from scratch, setting out to create an object that inspired emotion and enthusiasm, a design that was everyday yet not ordinary, a car that communicated choice rather than conformity.

The Cube's objectives are clear: functional, flexible and personal. The Cube makes a bold stand against our cultural obsession with speed, inviting owners to slow down and take life at a more restful pace. Like a modernist sculpture, a cubist painting or a piece of contemporary architecture, the car has been designed to inspire contemplation. From the gentle curves that form the edges of the car's space-efficient bodywork to a cosseting cabin that doubles up as a mobile living space, the Cube confounds conventional wisdom.

Just as cubist art fractured the surface of paintings and sculptures to reveal a multiplicity of views, so the Nissan Cube turns automotive design on its head, exploding stereotypes and forging a new way of looking at the city car.
www.cubelist.com

cube
design by nissan

REPORTS

DESIGN IN BUSINESS

ADDING CREATIVE VALUE

In our new section, we talk to five company leaders working at the intersection of design and business. While active in different sectors, in today's economic climate they naturally share a common preoccupation. In the words of DURAVIT CEO Franz Kook: 'It's all about more design value for less money.' Adding value may mean making more sustainable products, like PHILIPS Consumer Luminaires, or collaborating with artists, like HI-MACS and KVADRAT, with students, like LEOLUX, or with architects, like DURAVIT. The direction may vary, but design is always in the driving seat.

+ **AIMING HIGH:** THE ART OF HI-MACS
+ **HOUSE STYLE:** DURAVIT & PABLO KATZ
+ **FIREWORKS:** KVADRAT & ROMAN SIGNER
+ **RAY OF LIGHT:** PHILIPS AND THE LATEST LEDS
+ **SYNERGY:** THE LEOLUX WAY

AT THE THOMAS DEMAND EXHIBITION, HOSTED
BY THE NATIONAL GALLERY IN BERLIN IN 2009, LUXURIOUS
DRAPERY COVERING A HIDDEN FRAMEWORK FORMED
THE BACKGROUND FOR DEMAND'S PHOTOGRAPHS.

ADVOCATE OF THE ARTS

**KVADRAT's cooperation with artists like Thomas Demand and
Olafur Eliasson has made CEO ANDERS BYRIEL passionate about art.**

WORDS **FEMKE DE WILD**
PHOTOS **COURTESY OF KVADRAT**

When did you start doing art projects?
The art projects actually developed on
their own, through word of mouth. In 2004
we were introduced to Thomas Demand,
who was working on a big solo exhibition
in Bregenz at the time. Thomas was
very excited about textiles and ended up
making a small cinema out of upholstery
for the show. Designer Aamu Song had
contacted us earlier about her Reddress
project. We didn't think of communication
or public relations; we just wanted to
realize her ideas. Then Thomas introduced
us to Rosemarie Trockel, to whom we
donated 1.2 tonnes of wool for *Yes, but,*
a work of art featured at her Post-
Menopause exhibition. Again through
friends of friends, Olafur Eliasson came

along. And Alfredo Häberli introduced
me to Roman Signer.
What interested you in these projects?
Our primary audience consists of
architects and designers – people
constantly in search of inspiration – and
contemporary art is one of the places they
can find it. Art poses questions. Art allows
you to push the envelope and do things that
haven't been done before. If you have an
impact on contemporary art, it spills over
into architecture. So we like to see textile
integrated with art. We want to delve into
the borderland between disciplines.
Is art the only way to explore this borderland?
We're taking two approaches. Art projects
are one way, and the other is the creation
of inspiring showrooms and installations.

With the Bouroullec brothers, for example,
we're working on pushing the boundaries
of design and on inventing new typologies.
You can push the boundaries in art, design
or technology – the idea is the same, but
the direction taken is different in each case.
It's all about not underestimating our
clients and our audience. I see the art
projects as something we definitely have
to keep doing. It's getting more and more
exciting.
**Like the recent Thomas Demand exhibition at
the Neues Museum in Germany?**
The exhibition took place in the last
building that Mies van der Rohe realized in
Berlin. The combination between Mies and
Demand was almost mythical. Being part
of re-creating such a special space

FROM A DANISH BEACH LAST SUMMER, SWISS ARTIST ROMAN SIGNER FIRED EXPLOSIVES, TO WHICH HE HAD ATTACHED 50 M OF RED FABRIC BY KVADRAT – A BRIGHT STREAMER THAT FORMED A FLEETING ARC ABOVE THE NORTH SEA.

'I see art as a contribution to progress – to moving ahead'
Anders Byriel

is amazing. Demand used 4.5 km of heavy upholstery fabric. He covered big wooden frames with textile and hung them with infinite perfection. Thomas's pictures were mounted in the space. Mies liked textiles, and he used them in his buildings, frequently from floor to ceiling.

Do you brief the artists you work with?
We never brief them. Roman Signer's project is a good example. As a big admirer of his work, I think he is underestimated. This was the first time Roman had worked with a company like ours. We waited for him for weeks, and I had no clear idea of what he wanted to do. When he finally arrived, he had a box of explosives sent from Hamburg, which I had to keep in my office for days. We had a rather vague

conversation about doing something in the city, but he ended up choosing the beach for his happening – the perfect location.

It sounds as if you have a personal fascination with art.
It's turned into a fascination. I was raised around modernist art and architecture, and I've visited almost all the modernist museums in Europe. They are very interesting, but I didn't feel that what I saw was really relevant. Realizing that contemporary art *is* relevant for me – as a person living at this particular time – was a breakthrough. Being with people like Thomas and Olafur has strengthened this belief. The deeper you delve into contemporary art, the more addictive it becomes.

Why is contemporary art more relevant than modernism?
We are more complicated people in 2009 than we were in 1952. The world is more complex. There's more mental noise, so you have to make different art. I believe the best art is inclusive – it sucks you in and has lots of layers. Olafur's work is a good example. The superficial level is democratic and easy to understand, but as you go deeper, you discover many, many levels. Thomas's work is quite layered too.

More and more artists are being asked to design interiors. Will you ask artists to design your showrooms as well?
I wouldn't rule it out. I've actually tried to persuade Thomas, but it hasn't worked out yet. Some people firmly believe >>>

'Art can inspire designers to be brave'
Anders Byriel

IN 2005 KOREAN DESIGNER AAMU SONG CREATED REDDRESS, AN ENORMOUS GOWN FOR WHICH SHE USED 550 M OF KVADRAT FABRIC: SONG'S CHERRY-RED 'TENT' CAN ACCOMMODATE A PERFORMER AS WELL AS A SMALL AUDIENCE.

that artists and designers should each do their own thing, but it would get pretty boring if everybody stuck to one discipline. We want to encourage new ways of using textiles in architecture. Textiles give spaces tactility and a human touch. We're proud of how this idea has been integrated into our London showroom. The project's been criticized because it looks cold at first sight, but look closer and you'll see that textiles play a nurturing role there. It's an example of art inspiring designers to be brave.

Where does art fit into your marketing strategy?
It's part of our strategy, but it's not a marketing trick. Our strategy is to be a very strong business in terms of culture.

We thrive on culture. If you want to be part of Kvadrat, work with Kvadrat or be related to Kvadrat, you have to be interested in the cultural aspect of our activities. I see art as a contribution to progress – to moving ahead. It's a way to inspire our audience, but it's also the fuel that propels our employees. Art motivates us, and that's the primary reason we're involved in it. I believe in the comfort factor of good salaries and benefits, but content is everything. We take this extremely seriously.

Has the credit crunch influenced the situation at Kvadrat?
We're a family business. We're here for the long run, and a little bit of turbulence has no effect on our goals. Things have slowed

down a bit, but we're still making a profit. We haven't cut down on expenses to any great degree. And we continue to invest in the art projects; it's a great way to keep the energy flowing. We'll be involved in projects like these for the next 20 years – what you've seen is only the beginning. ∎

KVADRAT DONATED 1.2 TONNES OF WOOL TO ROSEMARIE TROCKEL
FOR POST-MENOPAUSE, THE EXHIBITION SHE MOUNTED
AT MUSEUM LUDWIG IN COLOGNE, GERMANY.

ANDERS BYRIEL.

KVADRAT

WEBSITE kvadrat.dk
LOCATION Ebeltoft (DK)
ESTABLISHED 1968
AREA OF DISTRIBUTION Worldwide
ANNUAL TURNOVER (2008) € 67.4 million
MARKET SECTOR Textiles
BEST-KNOWN PRODUCTS Hallingdal, North Tiles
and Clouds
BEST-SELLING PRODUCT Hallingdal
COLLABORATING DESIGNERS Alfredo Häberli, Peter Saville,
Akira Minagawa, Tord Boontje, Ronan and Erwan Bouroullec,
David Adjaye, Olafur Eliasson, Nanna Ditzel, Finn Sködt
and many more
AWARDS Wallpaper Design Award for Most Innovative
Textile 2009 for Clouds (Ronan and Erwan Bouroullec),
Innovationspreis Architektur Textil Objekt 2009 for Village
(Alfredo Häberli), AIT Award Architecture Textile 2009
for Highfield and Village (Alfredo Häberli),
Forum AID Award 2007 for North Tiles
(Ronan and Erwan Bouroullec)

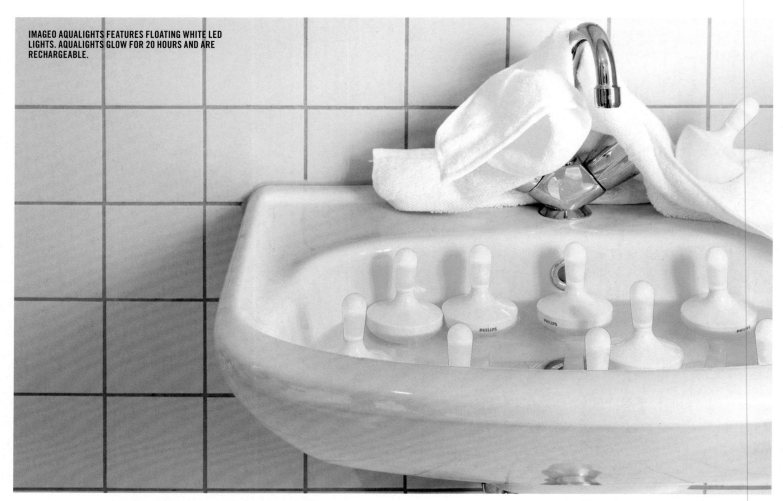

IMAGEO AQUALIGHTS FEATURES FLOATING WHITE LED LIGHTS. AQUALIGHTS GLOW FOR 20 HOURS AND ARE RECHARGEABLE.

IN A DIFFERENT LIGHT

With the end of the conventional light bulb in sight, PHILIPS CONSUMER LUMINAIRES' design director PAUL BAS talks about the future of light.

WORDS **FEMKE DE WILD**
PHOTOS **COURTESY OF PHILIPS**

In Europe, the fate of the light bulb was sealed with a definitive flourish last year. While consumers desperately stockpile the incandescent bulbs that have served humanity well for over two centuries, lighting manufacturers are trying to develop – and eventually market – the ideal alternative. Examples include Philips' latest LED solutions, which the company installed in a room of Amsterdam's Lloyd Hotel as part of the city's recent Inside Design event. A good reason to ask Paul Bas, design director of Philips Consumer Luminaires, to share his vision of the future with us.

It's fair to say that Philips has the soon-to-vanish light bulb to thank for its tremendous success. How do you feel about that?
Although the incandescent light bulb produces what we regard as beautiful light, it simply isn't the most eco-friendly source of light, and Philips maintains an ongoing awareness of sustainability. And the demise of the light bulb isn't just about loss; LEDs offer completely new possibilities, both visual and technological. The 'D' in LED stands for diode – a very tiny object. Considering its minuscule size, the amount of light produced by a high-power LED is gigantic.
Can you tell us more about these new possibilities?
LEDs have a number of advantages.

The most important is the integration of everything into one luminaire. Instead of separate fittings and separate light bulbs, we'll be marketing fully integrated solutions. The entire interface of a fitting is no longer necessary. This gives designers a wealth of freedom, although perhaps not quite as much as some people think. Like light bulbs, LEDs generate heat. A lot of engineering skill is needed if you want to guarantee their long life. What's more, the technology needed to make LEDs into functional light sources – such as lenses and other optical devices – still takes up quite a bit of space. We're expecting that aspect of LED light to become less and less expensive in the future, however. Then, too, because some of today's LEDs can keep

THE NESTOR FLOOR LAMP, WHICH BELONGS TO THE LIRIO COLLECTION, IS EQUIPPED WITH PHILIPS' ECOHALO HALOGEN BULBS.

ANOTHER MEMBER OF THE LIRIO FAMILY, THE WALTZ CHANDELIER, IS AVAILABLE IN BLACK OR WHITE. THE LUMINAIRE IS EQUIPPED WITH FIVE G9 ECOHALO 28W HALOGEN BULBS.

PAUL BAS.

PHILIPS

WEBSITE philips.com
LOCATION Eindhoven (NL)
ESTABLISHED 1920s; first dedicated design department: 1960
AREA OF DISTRIBUTION Worldwide
ANNUAL TURNOVER (2008) € 5.6 billion
MARKET SECTOR Healthcare, lifestyle and lighting
BEST-KNOWN PRODUCTS Philips incandescent bulb, Wake-up light, Senseo coffee machines, Philishave electric shaver, Sonicare toothbrush, LivingColors, Aurea television
BEST-SELLING PRODUCTS Depends on the country in question

A FROSTED WHITE TABLE MODEL, PART OF THE PHILIPS LIVINGCOLORS COLLECTION, STANDS ON THE SHELF OF A BOOKCASE AT THE LLOYD HOTEL. STYLING BY KAMER465.

working for an average of 15 to 25 years, we will be able to make products that will last even longer than the ones we're manufacturing at the moment.

All well and good, but recently doubts have arisen about the allegedly 'environmentally friendly' reputation of LEDs.
You have to look at energy consumption from an integral perspective. Producing a car that uses 10 per cent less energy is daft. Taking into account all the energy needed to manufacture a car, you can never come out on top. Saving up to 80 per cent by using LEDs, however, results in a real benefit. Philips is certainly not investing in anything that won't live up to long-term expectations.

A lot of designer lamps rely completely on the old-fashioned bulb. Nobody seems willing to abandon this tried-and-true light source.
This has to do with the quality of the light. The colour temperature of an LED isn't yet optimal when compared with that of a conventional incandescent bulb or halogen bulb. It's still too cool for most people's liking. Other energy-saving light bulbs already produce a more pleasing light temperature, but they can't all be dimmed yet. They have a different light spectrum, and they behave differently. When the filament of a conventional bulb gets hot, the quality of the illumination produced is very much like that of candlelight. We're using new technologies to create light in a completely different way, resulting in a totally different feeling

and a new type of experience. People may find it strange at first, but it has its advantages.

Such as?
Scientists have shown that some LED lights produce better colour rendering than the conventional light bulb. The colours you see outside on an overcast day, for example, are rendered perfectly. In truth, the incandescent bulb isn't ideal, because the light it emits is too orange and yellow. The light from LEDs will be closer to sunlight, but we'll need some time to get used to it.

Isn't a search for a good substitute for the light bulb at the top of your agenda?
Philips just submitted an entry to a competition for the L Prize. Entrants are asked to design the kind of alternative you've mentioned. It has to satisfy standards with respect to colour rendering, light efficiency and energy consumption. Participants are asked to supply the U.S. Department of Energy with a couple of thousand samples to prove that the light source can be massproduced. Philips was first in line, which should confirm the importance we place on finding a substitute for the conventional light bulb. We're not talking about an instant replacement for the entire industry, but ultimately – don't ask me when – the light bulb will have a certain value as an antique. I expect integrated solutions to fully take over the market.

What do such solutions look like?
The trend among today's designers

is to create very flat, slimline products that show how tiny LEDs are. It's true that we're able to work with different proportions than we once were, but we also have to pursue a new dimension in which we use LEDs more for their intrinsic – and less for their extrinsic – properties. Integration can lead to completely new lighting applications: solutions that are based not on technology, but on new experiences you want to offer the customer. There's not much I can tell you, because we're still in the research stage, and I don't want to give anything away.

Just a little hint?
You've got developments in technology, and you've got users. Our job is to bring the two together. Take the iPhone. In the past, people couldn't have imagined that they'd ever *want* to do so many things with a single device. As a lighting designer, you need to intuit where such sensitivities lie – to recognize what might actually enhance everyday life and to figure out how to create a symbiotic relationship between light and user.

An interesting time for lighting designers, isn't it?
I feel privileged to be working in the industry at a time in which such an enormous change is taking place. Until a few years ago, my colleagues and I were forced to work with a limited number of light sources. Now we're being asked how big to make the LEDs for certain designs. It's a whole new world. ■

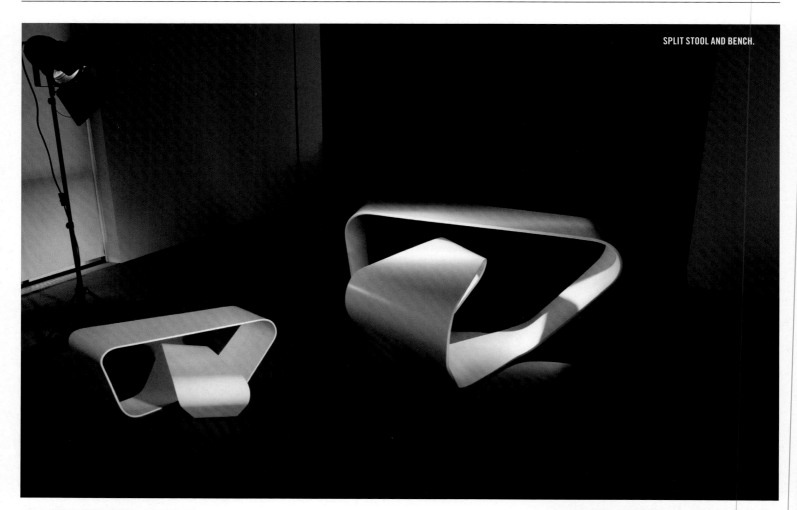

SPLIT STOOL AND BENCH.

SPOT ON

For the London Design Festival, Philip Michael Wolfson created a vanitas-style exhibition, Desaturated Dogmas, for HI-MACS. Vice president FREDERIC WILLAME explains why.

WORDS **MEREL KOKHUIS**
PHOTOS **COURTESY OF HI-MACS**

Why did HI-MACS decide to do an installation at The Dock?
We actually had a HI-MACS stand at 100% Design as well, as our main intention was to create 'design circuits' throughout the city with different events and exhibitions. The Dock installation was a partnership with designer Philip Michael Wolfson and manufacturer UK Solidity.

What did HI-MACS want to achieve with this presentation?
For us, collaboration with an important designer like Wolfson represents the meeting point between high-end design and a new-generation material like HI-MACS Natural Acrylic Stone, a product that offers endless possibilities for architects, designers and manufacturers.

But why Wolfson rather than another designer?
HI-MACS is eager to support and collaborate with creative people. The style of Wolfson's projects is in perfect harmony with what HI-MACS has to offer. In this case, he designed both the stand and the products presented. Wolfson's unique approach to design is inspired by the dynamics of fracture and fragmentation and the manipulation of fluid forms, which explore and redefine the human perception of solid materials. The presentation showcased Wolfson's new HI-MACS products, a collection of five pieces of furniture: Eruption, Omni, Split, Twisted and Why Not.

What went on at the briefing?
The project was initiated by Chris Cook,

the founder of Solidity Ltd. Tom Dixon provided us with an exhibition space at The Dock, the heart of his contribution to the London Design Festival and a venue that was organized in conjunction with Derwent London. Cook contacted Wolfson, and together they offered to work with our products. Within a very short time, we had agreed on half a dozen pieces, which Solidity made for the event.

Can you describe the design concept?
The idea behind Desaturated Dogmas was an environment of fantasy and creation. The monochromatic 'stage sets' allowed for a personal interpretation of colour, event and place. The inspiration for these sets came from symbolic 17th-century still-life paintings known as *vanitas*,

TWISTED DESK.

WHY NOT MIRROR.

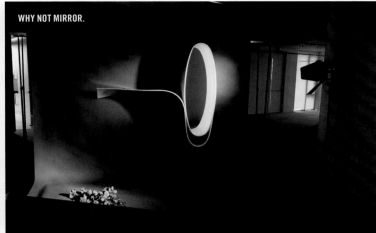

TWISTED DESK.

**'Our main intention was
to create "design circuits"
throughout the city'**
Frederic Willame

FREDERIC WILLAME.

with their focus on mortality, knowledge, the immateriality of earthly life and the transient nature of vanity. Counterpoints were a couple of sets that referenced transformation and resurrection. A single bright daub of paint supplied the only colour. Spotlights picked out the products, and an accompanying soundtrack was made for the exhibition.

Did you have a particular reason for choosing this concept?
Our most important reason was to rid HI-MACS of its industrial and commercial connotation as a material used exclusively for bathrooms and kitchens. We wanted to elevate it to the level of a 'noble' material in a neutral setting. To achieve our goal, we aimed for an environment more

representative of a gallery presentation than a trade show. 'Still life' stage sets, soundtrack and lighting were all part of generating the desired atmosphere. ∎

HI-MACS

WEBSITE himacs.eu
LOCATION Geneva (CH) and Seoul (KR)
ESTABLISHED 2002
AREA OF DISTRIBUTION Europe
MARKET SECTOR Interior and exterior (surface) materials
BEST-KNOWN PRODUCT LG Electronic
BEST-SELLING PRODUCT LG Mobile Phone
COLLABORATING DESIGNERS Zaha Hadid, Jean Nouvel, Ron Arad, David Chipperfield Architects, Marc Newson and many more

PROTOTYPE OF
LOTTE DOUWES'
PROJECT.

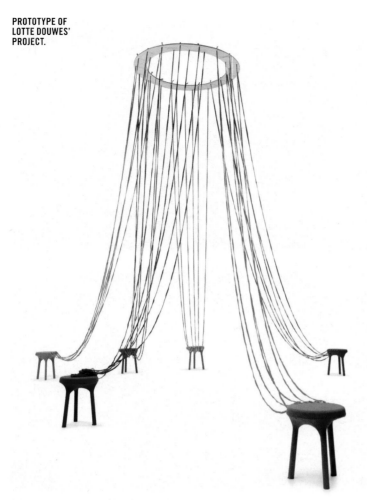

PROTOTYPE OF RACHEL GRIFFIN
AND ELKE VAN DEN BERG'S
NAKED PROJECT.

IN THE FRONT SEAT

Dutch company LEOLUX has some original ways to convey its unique selling point –
its manufacturing expertise – explains CEO FRANK VAN WERKUM.

WORDS **MEREL KOKHUIS**
PHOTOS **COURTESY OF LEOLUX**

Currently celebrating its 75th birthday, Leolux is an essentially Dutch company recognized worldwide for the high quality and ergonomic comfort of its leather seating elements. Since Frank van Werkum – previously associated with Vescom and De Ploeg – arrived in 2007, he's implemented an ongoing series of small changes. Van Werkum maps out the course he's set for Leolux and explains the rationale behind his decisions.

When you arrived at Leolux, what was your main objective?
Leolux is one of the largest factories in northern Europe producing design furniture. We have 500 employees, as opposed to our competitors, who have an average of 30. We do everything ourselves,

from constructing the wooden frames to putting the finishing touches on the end product. We operate a paintwork factory and a transport division. We make and upholster all the frames. We have our own showrooms. I realized there was practically nothing I could do to improve the company. My job was to find a way to emphasize its strong points. To focus more and more on the core business.

And those strong points would be . . . ?
High quality, comfort and independence – we don't have to rely on outside sources. We use the finest leathers and put great stock in our ergonomic design. Functionality is just as important as aesthetics. That's why our slogan is 'making sitting a pleasant experience'.

How have you managed to accentuate Leolux's strong points?
By paying attention to detail. And by solidifying the company's prime position within the 'making industry'. As I've said, we're one of the few furniture companies that still have in-house facilities for making everything. Because the whole idea is so interesting, we wanted to share it with people. In September 2007 we opened a visitors centre for this very purpose, called Via Creandri. Our guests have the opportunity to follow the entire manufacturing process of a piece of Leolux furniture from start to finish.
What else have you been doing?
We noticed that despite the glut of young design talent around, these people

ELKE VAN DEN BERG AND RACHEL GRIFFIN PRESENT THEIR DESIGNS AT LEOLUX IN VENLO.

STAND AT THE HOME FURNITURE FAIR, WOONBEURS AMSTERDAM 2009, WHERE THE PROJECT WAS EXHIBITED.

LOTTE DOUWES PRESENTS HER DESIGNS AT LEOLUX.

PRESENTATION OF LOTTE DOUWES' WORK AT THE FINAL ASSESSMENT.

'Women know best what consumers want'
Frank van Werkum

frequently have trouble selling their work. In many cases, they know so little about the manufacturing process that they design furniture which is nearly impossible to make. Nor do they give much thought to marketing methods. As a result of serving on the jury for the René Smeets Prize, I had good contacts with the Design Academy Eindhoven, and I suggested to the academy that we combine forces.

Can you explain your joint venture with the Design Academy Eindhoven in greater detail?
There are a lot of talented students at the Design Academy, and I wanted to help them. Instructors at the school asked their students to come up with an imaginary

subsidiary for Leolux and to make a suitable design for it. Although their designs didn't have to be anything like our leather furniture, they did have to be manufactured in our factory.
The project gave these students a chance to make get to know the 'making industry' and make good prototypes.

What happened to the prototypes?
We offered the best designs a public platform – a selection of the student work appeared at the Home Furniture Fair in Amsterdam. We'll be showing these prototypes in Kortrijk, Milan and Cologne as well. And we have some 700 dealers who wouldn't mind hosting temporary exhibitions of these designs in their showrooms.

Sounds as though the students at DAE really benefited from this project.
Absolutely. Besides having a chance to make good prototypes, they also had the opportunity to make use of our employees' know-how. Rather than stagnating in the concept stage, their designs were actually realized. And they also learned the best way to show their work to the public.
And did Leolux benefit from the collaboration as well?
We like the idea of gathering together a team of good designers. Although we may not do anything with these particular prototypes, there's still the possibility of approaching one or more of the designers for the development of a new project at some future date. Or we might use one >>>

CAMPING IN UNBEARABLE LUXURY, BY DENNIS PARREN, DURING THE FINAL ASSESSMENT.

'Young design talents frequently have trouble selling their work'
Frank van Werkum

PROTOTYPE OF DENNIS PARREN'S FOLD-UP SOFA, PRODUCED BY LEOLUX.

of their other designs as a styling prop for our brochure.

Any other special attempts to draw attention to Leolux?
Together with the stylists at Kamer 465, we've made sure that photographs of our furniture focus more on the detailing. We're now showing, for instance, that high-tech resources can be combined flawlessly with traditional craftsmanship – an unusual but powerful union. Leolux furniture is known for attention to detail and a perfectly finished appearance. Not long ago someone remarked that our chairs look just as good from the back as they do from the front. For this reason, quite a few people have treated our seating elements as objects, putting them in the middle of the

room rather than against a wall. We're also working with a gallery that's compiling a collection of art for us. We've been using the pieces in this collection for photo shoots, because we like the idea of linking Leolux to art. Art and design are both the result of creative processes that share a need for craftsmanship in their realization.

Have you changed anything within the company itself?
My main effort there has been to add more women to the staff, and I've got plenty of reasons for doing so. Women know best what customers want. At least 80 per cent of consumer purchasing is down to choices made by women. They have good taste; they have a 'double purse' – their own and their husband's; and, finally, they look with their

hands. They appreciate quality. Our policy on communication is aimed primarily at women. Other changes include employing someone who's involved in the colour aspect of furniture design, expanding the team with a genuine leather specialist and, more recently, bringing a designer on board to help us develop our trade-fair stands to the next level.

What are your plans for the future?
Not long ago we set up a Leolux subsidiary called Pode. Furniture marketed under this name is just as good as, but more affordable than, the pieces in the Leolux collection. Our target group consists of young people with good taste and modest means. We can keep costs low by offering a limited number of options, using less

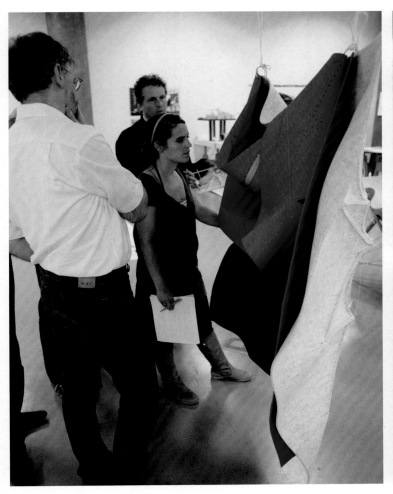

FINAL ASSESSMENT
OF JONAS LUTZ'S ARMCHAIR
PENNA AT DESIGN ACADEMY
EINHOVEN.

TUTOR BAS VAN TOL AND LEOLUX'S HEAD
OF PRODUCT DEVELOPMENT, HENK JEGERS,
ASSESSING ELISE VAN MOURIK'S ARMCHAIR.

LEOLUX'S HEAD OF PRODUCT DEVELOPMENT, HENK JEGERS
EXAMINES THE PENNA ARMCHAIR BY JONAS LUTZ.

FRANK VAN WERKUM.

PROTOTYPE OF ELISE VAN MOURIK'S
ARMCHAIR, PRODUCED BY LEOLUX.

expensive fabrics and manufacturing larger volumes. And we've decided not to spend a fortune on marketing. At the moment, we have a hundred dealers in the Benelux. Our goal is to continue growing. As far as short-term projects are concerned, this week I'll be going to Milan with a couple of colleagues to gather inspiration. We have no fixed plan; we're just going to let all the lovely things we see make their impact. Shoes, bonbons, packaging – any shape, colour or material has the potential to spark a new idea. ∎

LEOLUX

WEBSITE leolux.com
LOCATION Venlo (NL)
ESTABLISHED 1934
AREA OF DISTRIBUTION Worldwide
ANNUAL SALESTURNOVER €120 million
MARKET SECTOR Design furniture
BEST-KNOWN PRODUCT Pallone (design: Boonzaaijer/ Mazairac/De Scheemaker, 1989)
BEST-SELLING PRODUCTS Cuno (design: Cuno Frommherz, 2008), B Flat (Andreas Berlin, 2005), Vol de Rêve (Jane Worthington, 2006), Parabolica (Stefan Heiliger, 2008)
COLLABORATING DESIGNERS Jane Worthington, Hugo de Ruiter, Andreas Berlin, Cuno Frommherz, Gabriele Assmann, Norbert Beck, Frans Schrofer, Braun & Maniatis, Stefan Heiliger, Jan Armgardt

FROM THE BATHTUB IN THE MASTER BEDROOM, YOU HAVE A VIEW OF THE OUTDOORS.

CLEAN LINES

According to CEO FRANZ KOOK of DURAVIT, the products used in a Pablo Katz-designed, eco-friendly house near Paris are meant 'to set an example'.

WORDS **FEMKE DE WILD**
PHOTOS **ARNAUD RINUCCINI**

In a suburb sometimes referred to as 'the countryside of Paris', Hélène and Laurent (who asked that their full names not be used) recently built their eco-friendly dream house, Magic Cube CK06, which was designed by French-Argentine architect Pablo Katz. The project was supported by Duravit, which supplied sanitaryware for the house. CEO Franz Kook talks about the importance to manufacturers, in their attempts to reach the end user, of both small-scale local and large-scale international projects.

Why did Duravit support this project?
It's important to demonstrate your products in real-life situations and not only in showrooms. In the past, when architects needed sanitary appliances, they indicated only dimensions and quantities on their plans. They paid little attention to quality or design. Nowadays, we do our best to advise people and to point out all the possibilities. The owners of this house didn't want an ordinary bathroom. They had something really special in mind. And they were open to the idea of making the results public, at least to selected magazines. Magazines are often more willing to feature the design of a house than of a hotel, but hotel projects are yet another way to reach a new audience.

Hotel projects?
People who stay in modern hotels are noticing the gradual disappearance of a wall between the bedroom and the bathroom. You can separate the two areas if you want to, but they still form an entity. Some of the travellers who see this in their hotel rooms will be inspired to renovate their bathrooms at home. Duravit supplied Burj Dubai with 1,000 Starck vanity units, 7,000 toilets and bidets, and over 1,700 bath and whirl tubs. An enormous number of guests will see and use these products.

The house in France has an ecological design. Was that important to you?
The word 'sustainability' is influenced by inflation, so it's vital to demonstrate practical solutions. Water is reused in this house, and solar panels supply energy for heating water. The house has three baths, however, including one on the roof. It's an exaggeration to label the house as a totally sustainable building, but it does show that

A TRANSPARENT DOOR CAN BE CLOSED TO CREATE A PARTITION BETWEEN THE SHOWER AREA AND THE REST OF THE MASTER BEDROOM.

DURAVIT SUPPLIED SANITARYWARE FOR AN ECO-FRIENDLY HOUSE IN PARIS DESIGNED BY ARCHITECT PABLO KATZ.

FRANZ KOOK.

DURAVIT

WEBSITES duravit.de; duravit.nl; duravit.com
LOCATION Hornberg (DE)
ESTABLISHED 1817: earthenware products; sanitaryware: 1842
AREA OF DISTRIBUTION More than 90 countries worldwide
ANNUAL TURNOVER (2008) €335 million
MARKET SECTOR Sanitaryware, bathroom furniture, wellness products and accessories, kitchen sinks
BEST-KNOWN PRODUCTS Starck K by Philippe Starck, Sauna Inipi, BlueMoon, Sundeck
BEST-SELLING PRODUCT Starck 1 collection by Philippe Starck
COLLABORATING DESIGNERS Sieger Design, Philippe Starck, Michael Graves, Massimo Iosa Ghini, Phoenix Design, James Irvine, Lord Norman Foster, Frank Huster and Herbert Schultes, EOOS

'More design value for less money – that's the key to better living'
Franz Kook

---

it's possible to have a quality bathroom that doesn't consume an unnecessarily large amount of water and energy.

How can the design of sanitaryware contribute to sustainability?

We make sure our products use as little water as possible. Making toilets with a variety of flushing options helps, too, but the main thing is a manufacturing process that consumes a minimum of energy. Another contribution is a design with a timeless quality. We developed Starck 1 some 15 years ago, but it's still one of our major lines.

What do you consider most important: the project market or the consumer market?

When you have more than one child, you can't pick a favourite. We need both of

these markets. Projects have suffered as a result of the economic crisis, but at the same time we're seeing very strong growth in the middle classes of countries like India and China. It's these middle-class populations that need new, quality bathrooms. Renovation, on the other hand, is a prevailing activity in developed countries. Every ten years or so, hotels require renovation, and bathrooms in private residences should be replaced after about 20 years of use. What we're seeing, however, is a delay in renovation activities owing to the recession. People have quality products that are still functioning well despite their age. We have to wake up the market, create a demand for our products, and communicate the latest possibilities.

Don't you see a contradiction between designing sustainable products and creating a demand for new ones?

Yes, I do, but I'm talking about replacing a 20-year-old bathroom with a new one. Two decades is a long time. Installing a new bathroom at that point is a good investment. Quality of life is the most important issue here, and functionality is not enough to improve that quality. More design value for less money – that's the key to better living. ■

SUNSHADES & CURTAINS

KriskaDECOR

KRISKADECOR
BY JOSE MA SANS AMILL
Spain
info@kriskadecor.com
kriskadecor.com

Mini Longitude

SALT
England
enquiries@salt-uk.com
salt-uk.com

Cascade Coil 3/16"

CASCADE COIL DRAPERY
USA
draperysales@cascadecoil.com
cascadecoil.com

Siberian Larch
Exterior Shutters

NORMAN EUROPE
Netherlands
info@normaneurope.nl
normaneurope.nl

Xinghai

GKD
Germany
creativeweave@gkd.de
creativeweave.de

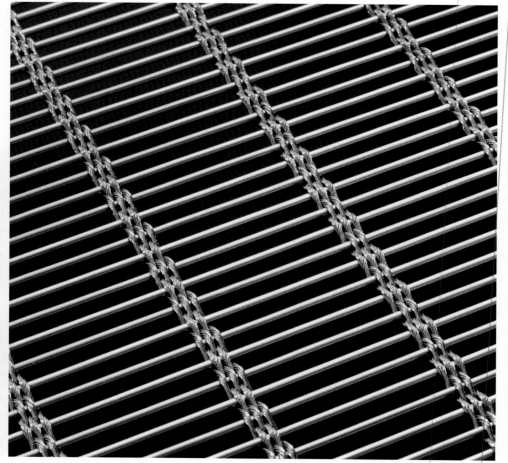

Wood Venetian Blind

BANDALUX
Spain
bandalux@bandalux.es
bandalux.com

Vivid

**BY MAJA JACOBSSON
LUDVIG SVENSSON**
Sweden
info@ludvigsvensson.com
ludvigsvensson.com

Summer Light

**BY FABRICIUS & GUNDERSEN
KURAGE**
Denmark
info@kurage.com
kurage.com

Ocean Master
MAX Classic

**BY DOUGAN CLARKE
TUUCI**
Netherlands
Info@tuuci.eu
tuuci.com

Baya

CLESTRA
France
info@clestra.com
clestra.com

Luxaflex Toolbox

LUXAFLEX BY HUNTER DOUGLAS
Netherlands
projecten@luxaflex-nederland.nl
luxaflex-projects.nl

YaZa Collection
BY LIBBY KOWALSKI
KOVA TEXTILES
USA
info@kovatextiles.com
kovatextiles.com

Parametre
SUNWAY
Netherlands
sunway@sunway.nl
sunway.nl

System W
BY CHRISTOPHE MARCHAND
ANN IDSTEIN
Sweden
info@annidstein.com
annidstein.com

Finespin
BY VALENTINA CALLUDRINI
MYCORE
Italy
inf@mycore.it
mycore.it

One Rail Sierra Papa Small

TWENTINOX
Netherlands
info@twentinox.com
twentinox.com

Intrepid

CORRADI
Italy
info@corradi.eu
corradi.eu

Wood Venetian Blinds

NORMAN EUROPE
Netherlands
info@normaneurope.nl
normaneurope.nl

Les Inattendues

BY JÉRÔME BRUNEEL
BISSON BRUNEEL
France
info@bisson-bruneel.com
bisson-bruneel.com

Roman Shade

BANDALUX
Spain
bandalux@bandalux.es
bandalux.com

Les Vegetales

BY JÉRÔME BRUNEEL
BISSON BRUNEEL
France
info@bisson-bruneel.com
bisson-bruneel.com

Small Details

The 2010 collection by CEBI offers both the freedom and the opportunity to choose from a wide variety of designs.

Design represents an endless world of alternatives, a world in which we encounter new things every day. Funnily enough, this world is also filled with limitations. It can be extremely difficult, for instance, to find design solutions that suit your personality. If you're looking for an elegant yet functional product that promises to reflect the inner you, it's time to take a good look at what Cebi has to offer.

Cebi – a company that operates worldwide – boasts a truly trendsetting production concept. For Cebi, it's not only the ideas and the designs that count, but also the way in which they are implemented. A great deal of skilled craftsmanship, aided by cutting-edge technology, goes into the realization of Cebi products. Cebi's reputation is based on prompt solutions for various needs and the firm's ability to offer a range of alternatives in short order. Every Cebi product that passes through quality control has been created to meet one or more challenges. ▬▬

Cebi Design
Turkey
cebi@cebidesign.com
cebidesign.com

DOOR HANDLES COLLECTION

The designs in Cebi's 2010 Door Handles Collection enliven metal surfaces and complement a wide variety of styles and tastes. Advanced technology goes into the production of these handles, which are manufactured according to high, internationally approved standards of quality that provide them with outstanding long-term functionality. Every manufacturing phase is accompanied by a thorough quality-control check. The resulting products are preferred for their durability and practicality. Cebi's rich, broad world of design is limited only by the user's imagination. It's a wonderful world, wide open to everyone's tastes and requirements.

CEBI DOOR HANDLES ADD A SPARK OF VITALITY TO ALL TYPES OF ENVIRONMENTS.

DETAILS OF THE JOY COLLECTION.

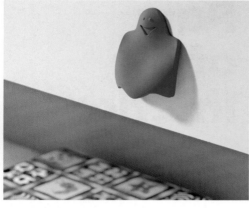

JOY COLLECTION

The designs in Cebi's 2010 Joy Collection include hundreds of attractive and amusing shapes and colours. The collection, which targets the younger generation in particular, is bright and cheerful. The practical, decorative designs are meant to pump extra energy into living areas occupied by young people. Children's health is of the utmost importance, so it goes without saying that Cebi's Joy Collection contains no harmful materials. What's more, all products in this high-tech range boast a 'soft touch' painted finish. These instant eye-catchers will surely appeal to youngsters – and to the young at heart – the world over.

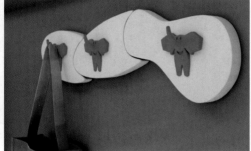

A SOPHISTICATED AESTHETIC MARKS CEBI'S HANDLES COLLECTION.

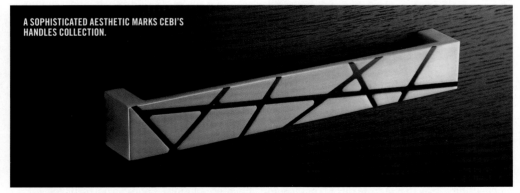

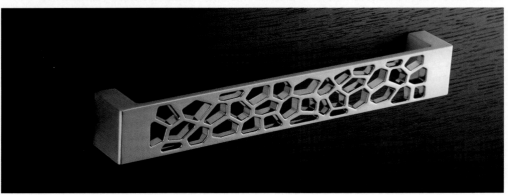

HANDLES COLLECTION

The designs in Cebi's 2010 Handles Collection add a spark of vitality to furniture and living spaces. The design of these handles – characterized by their strikingly sophisticated elegance – enhances the aesthetic of wood and metal surfaces. The manufacture of all Cebi handles is based on a series of careful calculations and refined combinations, which lead to products that adapt readily to the styles, materials and surfaces of all types of furniture.

Part of the Interior

VOGEL'S PRODUCTS audiovisual mounting solutions can be integrated into the interior in any number of stylish ways.

THE MOST POPULAR MODELS FOR HOTEL ROOMS ARE VOGEL'S WALL-MOUNTED SOLUTIONS.

Vogel's Products is Europe's leading manufacturer of innovative, top-quality mounting solutions for LCD and plasma TVs and monitors. Vogel's innovative range of brackets boasts unique features and unprecedented designs. The stylish design of these mounting systems has received recurrent recognition from the GIO, the IFA and others.

LCD and plasma screens are becoming an increasingly popular feature of not only home and office environments but also public venues. More and more often, hotels guests find LCD and plasma screens in their rooms instead of conventional television sets. Unlike products used in the home, professional displays are nearly always mounted on the wall or the ceiling, although floor models are also an attractive choice. For each of the many potential applications, Vogel's has designed a specific mounting solution for integrating the LCD

or plasma screen into the interior in an elegant manner. The result can be a welcome addition to the space that actually becomes part of the interior.

Vogel's TVskins are perhaps the most visible – or invisible – way to integrate an LCD or plasma screen into a public area. The TVskin is a custom housing for an LCD or plasma screen, but Vogel's can also supply a custom-designed housing that meets your specific requirements. A wide range of standard TVskins are available in every colour imaginable, including the exact shade needed to complement the interior in question. Ultimately, the screen is more than a separate accessory – thanks to Vogel's TVskin, it blends into its surroundings to merge with the interior.

Vogel's Products has introduced a new series of trolleys that allow for maximum flexibility. These trolleys can also be enhanced with a custom touch: Vogel's removable front covers,

which come in any colour or printed design and are easy to switch. Opt for a striking contrast, or create an air of subtle harmony.

The most popular models for hotel rooms are included in Vogel's broad selection of wall-mounted solutions. Choose from an array of super flat models, multi-adjustable models and remote-controlled adjustable models. All are characterized by clever innovative functions in combination with a stylish design. Vogel's Products mounting solutions are found in a wide range of locations, including airports, hotels, stations, conference rooms, shopping centres and restaurants. ■

Vogel's Products
Netherlands
info@vogels.com
vogels.com

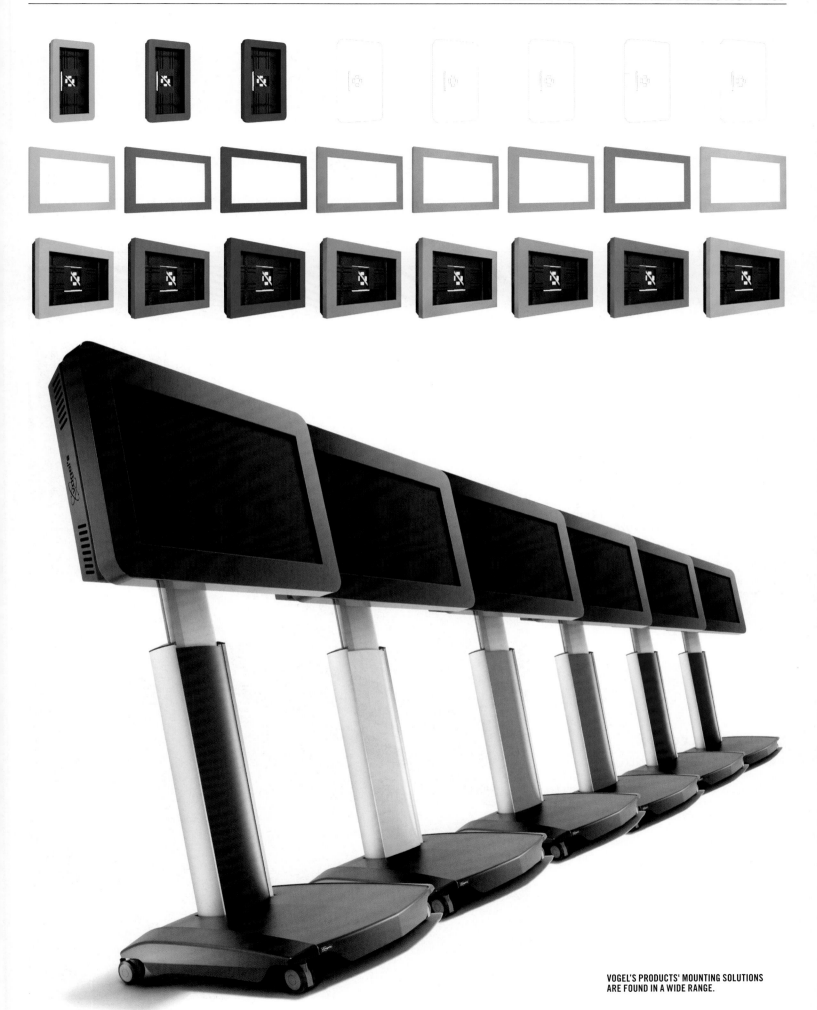

**VOGEL'S PRODUCTS' MOUNTING SOLUTIONS
ARE FOUND IN A WIDE RANGE.**

FLOR Plan

InterfaceFLOR's latest collection was designed to cause the least possible impact on the environment.

InterfaceFLOR's newest designs can be coordinated with one another, as well as with other InterfaceFLOR products for an interesting 'mix and match' of beautiful carpet tiles. 'The new collection – one of largest ever – reflects customer demand for versatility, durability and originality. It's been created to cause the least possible impact on the environment,' says Nigel Stansfield, senior director of product, design and innovation at InterfaceFLOR EMEAI.

Many of the new products have a high recycled content, made up of both post- and pre-consumer material, reflecting the company's commitment to closed-loop manufacturing. The tiles are also produced in accordance with the latest sustainable manufacturing processes, which generate a minimum of waste. Such methods are in keeping with InterfaceFLOR's Mission Zero ambition to be the world's first fully sustainable company by 2020. ▬

InterfaceFLOR
Europe
interface.nl@interfaceflor.eu
interfaceflor.eu

REPRISE COLLECTION

RePrise echoes the natural world in all its simple, effortless glory: from the characteristic patterns of tree trunks and bark to the rich, deep textures of the forest floor. Restore and Renew are both inspired by biomimicry. Boost your environmental credentials with carpeting that feature post-consumer and postindustrial recycled content in the yarn and postindustrial recycled content in the backing, important attributes of the company's Cool Carpet 'climate neutral' scheme. The random design allows for a non-directional installation, making the RePrise Collection even more flexible and cost-effective.

BOLD, BRIGHT AND ON-TREND, KEY FEATURES OFFERS CUSTOMERS A RANGE OF 20 VIBRANT COLOURS FOR CREATING THE PERFECT LOOK.

KEY FEATURES

Bold, bright and on-trend, Key Features offers customers 20 vibrant colours. Create the perfect look for any space, from an ultra-chic, fashionable restaurant to a busy, modern office designed to inspire creativity. But Key Features offers far more than just good looks. Strong, highly engineered fibres give these products their tough durability. The design, the highly textured surface and the choice of fabulous colours enables you to achieve that desired broadloom effect. Key Features is the definitive bold statement.

A HIGHLY TEXTURED SURFACE AND FABULOUS COLOURS MAKE KEY FEATURES THE DEFINITIVE BOLD STATEMENT.

REPRISE COMPLEMENTS AN INTERIOR WITH THE CHARACTERISTIC PATTERNS OF TREE TRUNKS AND BARK, AS WELL AS THE DEEP, RICH TEXTURES OF THE FOREST FLOOR.

WHEN YOU SELECT THE FLEXIBLE X-LOOP CARPET TILE, YOU CAN MATCH ANY COLOUR YOU CHOOSE.

X-LOOP

InterfaceFLOR wanted X-Loop to be sleek and distinctive, lightly patterned and shiny. The company drew inspiration for its contemporary, innovative carpet tile from both nature and the modern world. When InterfaceFLOR says X-Loop is totally flexible, they really mean it. With this mottled, metallic product, InterfaceFLOR can match any colour you choose: the only limit is your imagination. X-Loop comes in a wide range of colours; simply select the one that's right for you.

Heat of the Moment

In only five years, FREDDIE DIEPERINK and SANDER WINKELHUIS have built SAFRETTI into a successful producer of exclusive, ornamental fireplaces.

By sheer chance, Freddie Dieperink met Dutch interior designer Jan des Bouvrie five years ago on a flight to the international furniture fair in Milan. Their initial contact soon grew into a productive cooperative venture. The promotion and sales involved in this collaboration took place via indirect channels, such as interior designers and home-furnishing stores. On 1 January 2004, the Safretti trademark was registered.

Since then, top designers like Des Bouvrie, Roderick Vos, Henk Heres and Frans Schrofer have been creating beautiful fireplaces for Safretti, a brand that stands for exclusive design and environmentally friendly products. All Safretti fireplaces burn bio-alcohol, a 'green' fuel made from sugar beets. The fireplaces are equipped with 2-litre-capacity, bio-alcohol burners that operate, depending on the model, from six to ten hours. Thanks to the 100 per cent natural composition of the fuel, the fire from these products leaves no dark stains on ceiling or walls. There is no smoke, no soot and no scent, and thus no need for a flue or chimney. These decorative fireplaces can be mounted on (or integrated into) the wall quite easily. Cubico and Curva by Jan des Bouvrie are also attractive as freestanding objects. When you rearrange the furniture, just switch the position of the fireplace, too, if desired. And when you move house, the fireplace can simply be packed up and taken along.

Each of Safretti's ornamental fireplaces is handcrafted at the manufacturer's workshop in Haaksbergen. This is not an assembly-line operation, but a process marked by careful craftsmanship. 'We make about 3000 fireplaces a year here, which are distributed worldwide,' says Dieperink. 'We work with limited-edition designs – it's a way of guaranteeing exclusivity. We've shown our products at trade fairs throughout Europe and Asia, and the plan for next year is to cross the ocean to America. And to think that it all began with an idea and a chance encounter with Jan des Bouvrie on the way to Milan.' ■

Safretti
Netherlands
info@safretti.com
safretti.com

CARRÉ BL BLACK BY JAN DES BOUVRIE FOR SAFRETTI.

GAYA

A popular item from Safretti's winter collection 2008-2009 is Gaya, designed by Roderick Vos. At first sight, the fireplace looks like a framed, all-black painting. Vos's design trenscends the notion of a fireplace. In the wall panel of matte-black, powder-coated aluminium is a pouchlike protuberance that conceals 'Gaya's secret': the burner. As flickering flames enhance the interior, Gaya becomes a living work of art. This is a design reduced to pure simplicity – and one with a strong focus on the heart of the matter: fire.

CARRÉ AND DOUBLE VISION

Two other Jan des Bouvrie designs, Carré and Double Vision, are part of Safretti's latest collection. Serenity and simplicity are the key elements of the design of Double Vision. These fireplaces generate a timeless ambience and lay a foundation for creating a distinctive interior. The designs form an attractive symbiosis between two products that reinforce each other. 'My new fireplaces for Safretti add an extra dimension to the interior, thanks to their simplicity and to the play of lines,' says Jan des Bouvrie. Double Vision is available in white-framed or black-framed safety glass. The accompanying LCD screen, with integrated TV and radio, is available in two sizes: 37" HD Ready and 46" Full HD. It has two removable burners, each of which holds 2 litres of bio-alcohol.

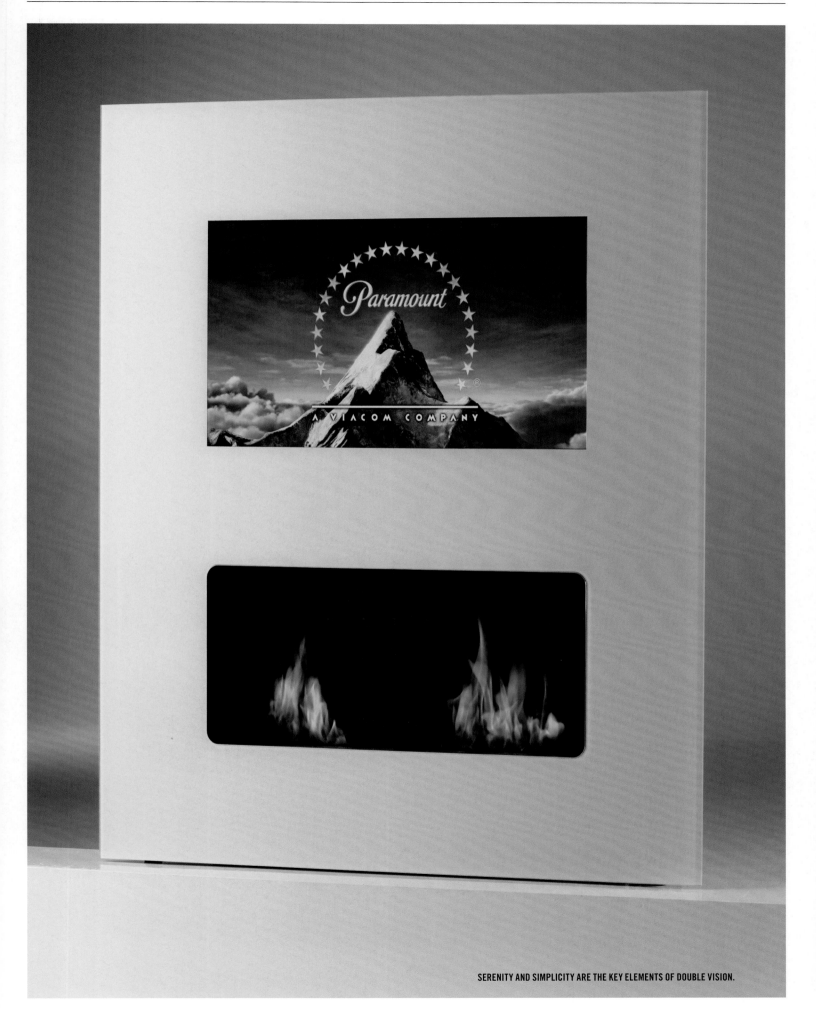

SERENITY AND SIMPLICITY ARE THE KEY ELEMENTS OF DOUBLE VISION.

'Designers can have a positive effect
on this collective hysteria; they can put
things in perspective again'
FRANÇOIS BERNARD

GOODS

MATERIAL MATTERS

FAIR PLAY

Our review of the European design-fair circuit of 2009 yields more than fantastic new products. From VIENNA – where MICHAEL YOUNG premiered his latest, industrially engineered works – to LONDON – where BENJAMIN HUBERT showcased new process-led pieces – the fair was a forum for experiment. It was heartening, too, to see design reflecting on itself, though the themes, events and exhibitions raised more questions than they answered. In PARIS, body-inspired objects queried design's role in our physical obsessions. In LISBON, design offices were explored through their daily routines, undermining the myth of effortless creativity.

BENJAMIN HUBERT.

GRADIENT, PART OF A COLLECTION FOR ERCOL.

HIGH-FLYING HUBERT

LONDON DESIGN FESTIVAL

A year after winning Blueprint's Most Promising Futures Designer award, BENJAMIN HUBERT arrived at the London Design Festival with a new batch of material- and process-focused work.

WORDS **GIOVANNA DUNMALL**
PHOTOS **COURTESY OF BENJAMIN HUBERT**

Your work focuses very much on material and process. What do you find so fascinating about the latter?
Process, whether it's glass-blowing or concrete-casting, informs the aesthetic and functionality of an object. Otherwise, you'd end up designing things that don't work with the material.

Do you visit manufacturers to learn about the techniques they employ?
I usually start by visiting the factory in question, together with the client, to get a better understanding of the process and the potential of the material involved. Because quite often people don't understand the material. When that happens, they try and get it do something that isn't possible.

Much of your lighting and furniture has a simple, clean aesthetic and a very solid look. Are you interested in durability and timelessness?
Yes, I'm interested in the idea of a product that lasts. I think that's part of what makes a design good or iconic.

While studying industrial design at Loughborough University, did you discover materials that seemed particularly attractive?
I worked with a glass-maker in my final year, and with a leather upholsterer. But most of my training has been in consumer goods – injection moulding, mobile phones, those kinds of things. They're still a part of what I do now and will certainly be an area of growth for me as my lighting and furniture designs establish themselves.

HEAVY DESK LIGHT, PART OF A COLLECTION
FOR DECODE LONDON.

ALL HUBERT'S PRODUCTS GROUPED TOGETHER.

CHIMNEY, A COLLECTION OF LAMPS FOR VIADUCT.

PEBBLE, PART OF A COLLECTION FOR DEVORM.

You're very young to be so successful, yet you make it look easy. Has it been easy?
No, and it still isn't. I think people underestimate how difficult it is. You can go off and make the prototypes and find manufacturers, and that's difficult enough. But as soon as you start working with a client, you're faced with a whole load of new challenges, expectations and timelines.

Clients haven't been a problem for you, have they?
I've talked to an awful lot of people over the past two years. I don't think a day goes by that I don't make an effort to introduce myself to somebody new. I've gone to trade fairs, walked into hundreds of stands, sat down with the right people and tried to get them interested. I probably get a hundred

no's for every yes, but if you can take that kind of rejection, this job isn't too bad.

You certainly are prolific. Don't you ever stop?
I'm pretty driven. Other people have said I'm prolific, too, but it's the only way you can make a living out of design. I say yes a lot, because I think that's the best approach. Even the smallest client represents an opportunity. ■

benjaminhubert.co.uk

WHO Benjamin Hubert
WHERE London
GOAL I'm still trying to establish my studio, which I'd like to be financially sound and respected in the industry for doing good design
LATEST PROJECT The coat stand for De La Espada, which was finished two days before the festival Approach Thorough and Innovative
PHILOSOPHY Essentially, it's about producing good design that is functional, visually appreciated and responsible from both an environmental and a social point of view

WHO Kyeok Kim
WHERE Seoul
GOAL Finding cultural value in a fusion of art and design
HOW Exhibiting my work and making my business grow
LATEST PROJECT The Re-connection of Objects
PHILOSOPHY I want to show the cultural value of work that combines art and design
APPROACH Currently, my work is based on the concepts of metamorphosis, mutation and transplantation

THE RE-CONNECTION OF OBJECTS IS COMPOSED OF VINTAGE CHAIRS, WAX, POLYURETHANE, ACRYLIC PAINT COMBINED WITH TEXTURE GEL, CERAMIC CUPS AND SOFT EPOXY RESIN.

KYEOK KIM.

BEST OF BOTH WORLDS

LONDON DESIGN FESTIVAL

Finery or furniture, functional or frivolous – at the London Design Festival, designer KYEOK KIM showed work that makes no distinction between the two.

WORDS **MEREL KOKHUIS**
PHOTOS **JEJU SIM**

How would you describe your style?
I call my work 'conceptual design' or 'design art'.

You went to school to learn jewellery design – so why furniture?
My jewellery designs led me to furniture quite naturally. In making a series of objects, I see each item as if it were a piece of jewellery that can be deconstructed and reconstructed. In this case the objects are ordinary chairs. Before creating them, I made illuminated pieces that relate to my wearable light jewellery. I'm trying to extend my area of expertise.

What's the concept behind The Re-Connection of Objects?
By deconstructing and reconstructing ordinary objects, I've reinterpreted the meaning of what it means to create. The

process of formation is part of the design. Each piece reveals its metamorphosis – its development as it was built and as I added a random array of things to it. The Re-Connection of Objects also refers to this translation or mutation of the original.

Where did you get the chairs and the teacups?
In Korea, you can buy vintage furniture in small-town shops. I restored the chairs and cups in some cases. I used a water-jet cutting machine to cut some of the cups. And after others had just come out of the kiln, I cut them and fired them again.

Why did you use chairs, teacups and spray foam?
Again, it was all about exploring concept and form through the deconstruction and reconstruction of everyday objects. And about reinterpreting the definitions of '

'to create' and 'to replace'. The original objects were just a starting point.

Did you design the chairs to sit on or to look at?
This must be the question I've been asked most often this week. Some of the chairs are to sit on and others are works of art. I'm planning to develop that line of thinking, as well as to work on materials and shapes that can be made into completely functional chairs.

What is your target group?
I want to make more limited-edition collections, so my main target at the moment is gallery owners. And collectors, of course.

What do you think you'd be if you weren't a designer?
A researcher. I like to analyse and write. ■
kyeokkim.com

THE ROCKING HOT DOG
DESIGNERS Nienke Klunder and Jaime Hayon
MATERIAL Fibreglass, aluminium, leather,
maple wood, chromed metal
DIMENSIONS 1500 x 370 x 730 mm (l x w x h)
PRICE €17,850 (£16,124)
LIMITED EDITION Eight pieces
GALLERY Spring Projects

LONDON DESIGN FESTIVAL

TYPE OF EVENT Festival
LOCATION London
NUMBER OF EXHIBITORS Around 170 partners take part
in the event
NUMBER OF VISITORS Estimated 300,000 at festival events
and a further million people at the public installations
TARGET GROUP Public, design professionals, international
visitors, students
DURATION 19 – 27 September
FREQUENCY Annually
WEBSITE FAIR londondesignfestival.com

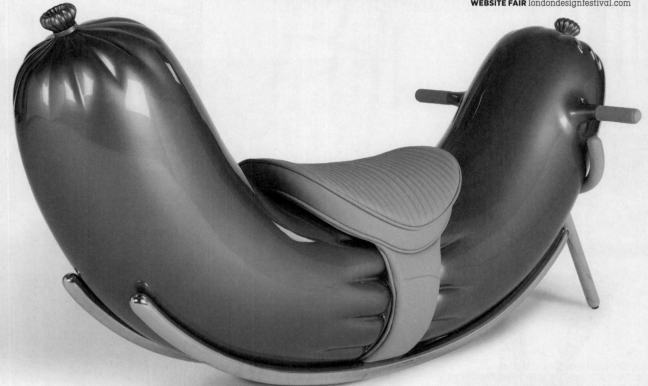

INTO THE SADDLE
LONDON DESIGN FESTIVAL

Despite the reference to pop culture, JAIME HAYON
and NIENKE KLUNDER's Rocking Hot Dog tastes
more like highbrow 'design art'.

WORDS **FEMKE DE WILD**
PHOTOS **COURTESY OF SPRING PROJECTS**

In September, Jaime Hayon and Nienke Klunder opened American Château Room One, an exhibition held at London gallery Spring Projects. Objects by both Hayon and Klunder shared the space with collaborative work, such as The Rocking Hot Dog. A gleaming purple frankfurter curves to fit its supporting metal frame. A saddle cinches the sausage halfway, suggesting that users, after lifting it away from the simple wooden stand at one end, can ride the bucking bronco.

A neutral review of The Rocking Hot Dog quickly leads to banalities, which may actually be the strong point of this work. It lacks the persuasive quality, however, of creations by the likes of Jeff Koons. The kitschy, prosaic hot dog obviously begs for a comparison to Koons, but Koons not only gave us 'originals'; he also knew

how to imbue his work with shock power. The Rocking Hot Dog is a cross between a semi-functional object and a work of art, a piece that explores the boundaries of the aesthetically correct and the socially acceptable, yet makes no lucid statement.

According to the gallery's press release, the designs on display 'are icons of the booming, fast-food American dream' and thus, like work by Koons, in the style of pop art. Pop artists borrowed images, often from American ad campaigns, which were labelled 'low art' by the cultural elite. Rather than opposing mass culture, they regarded it as a valuable source of material. Andy Warhol created reproducible work that cast doubt on the hand of the master, as well as on the 'uniqueness' of his or her art.

The Rocking Hot Dog also refers to a mass-

produced staple of the American lifestyle, but what Hayon and Klunder are trying to say remains unclear. Is the design a celebration of the banal? A criticism of the fast-food culture? Does the work investigate 'the elite notions of art and design'? Hayon – a child of the world of mass-production – had this piece manufactured by a company that makes Formula 1 chassis, thus elevating the design to the pricey sphere of the limited edition. Klunder and Hayon do just the opposite of what Warhol did, while choosing comparable icons. Their use of high-gloss materials and grand gestures smacks of highbrow 'design art' and takes the edge off the potentially interesting contrast between high and low art. ■

nienkeklunder.com, hayonstudio.com

THE NAKED EYE

MAISON & OBJET

Design doesn't get any edgier than BODY HOUSE,
a disquieting show of anatomically inspired pieces curated
by François Bernard for Maison & Objet.

WORDS **CHRIS SCOTT**
PHOTOS **COURTESY OF MAISON & OBJET**

AMONG THE STANDOUT PIECES WAS VLADI RAPPAPORT'S
TECHNICALLY ACCOMPLISHED SKULL CHAIR (RIGHT).

Three trend-forecasting agencies chose 'ReGeneration' as the theme for the autumn furniture fair in Paris, Maison & Objet. François Bernard, the director of one of these agencies, Croisements, used the human body to interpret the theme. The result was a fascinating show with an ample representation of the weird and the wonderful. Displayed at the 200-m2 Body House exhibition were some 70 objects and items of furniture, each inspired by some part of the human anatomy.

Why did you choose this subject?
It started with skin. I noticed that variations on the texture of skin were becoming more and more common in objects and furniture. Not only leather and suede, but also latex, rubber and soft-textured wood have been used to create an impression of skin, from baby-smooth to old and wrinkled, and in white, black and shades of tan. I was also inspired by Sakaya Yamamoto's tattooed latex 'skin,' Dejana Kabiljo's hair-upholstered seating and Ole Jensen's hot water bottles, which resemble human organs. I had never seen anything like these extraordinary objects, which indicate a whole new direction in design. Conventionally, the human body is rarely seen in the decorative arts.

The exhibition seems to reflect a contemporary obsession with the body.
You could write a book about the subject. Beginning in the 1960s, the most prominent means of cultural expression in Western societies has been 'me, me, me'.

The body has become the main instrument we use to express ourselves, both individually and collectively. Over a period of 20 to 30 years, we have seen the body move from expressing itself in art, sport, dance, yoga and fashion to being afraid of itself – afraid to grow old, to get fat, to smoke, to eat sugar – a shift underlined by anorexic models and an epidemic of plastic surgery.

Designers can have a positive effect on this collective hysteria. They can put things in perspective again. They can help us to see the body in ways unrelated to our current fascination and repulsion.

How did you handle the provocative nature of the theme?
I created an extremely simple white >>>

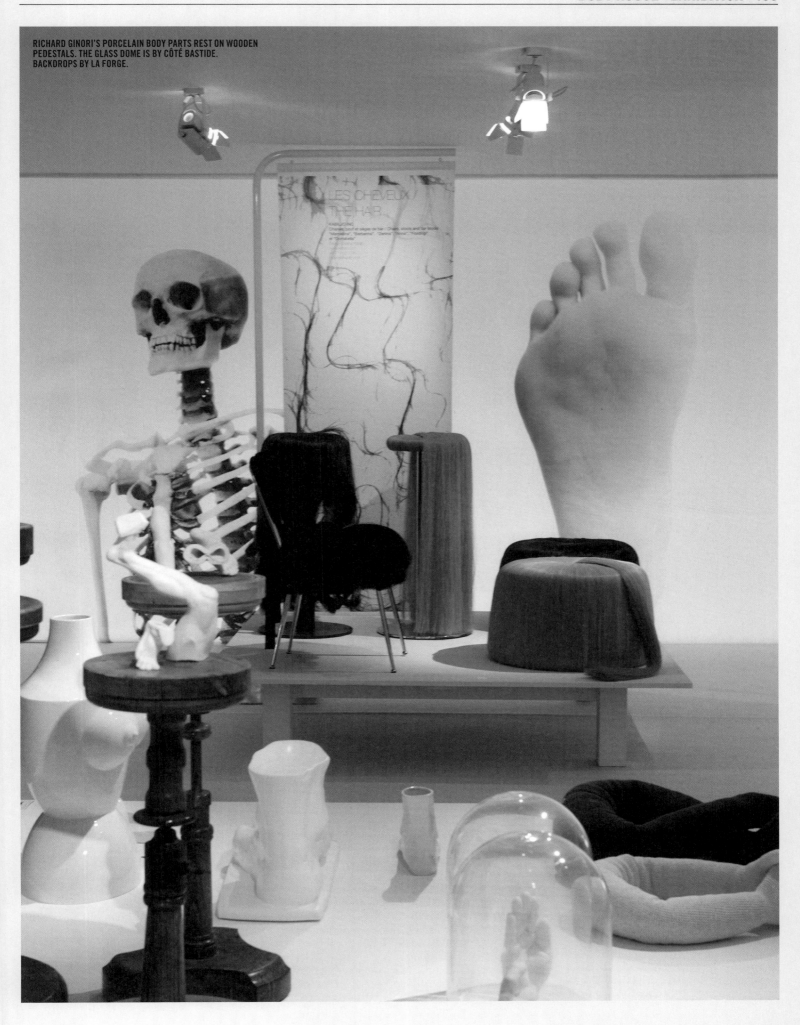

RICHARD GINORI'S PORCELAIN BODY PARTS REST ON WOODEN
PEDESTALS. THE GLASS DOME IS BY CÔTÉ BASTIDE.
BACKDROPS BY LA FORGE.

THE ALL-WHITE EXHIBITION SPACE ALLOWED THE OBJECTS TO SPEAK FOR THEMSELVES. LARGE BACKDROPS DEPICTING PARTS OF THE HUMAN BODY WERE DESIGNED BY LA FORGE.

setting, with low tables and signage explaining the different stages of research and creation pertaining to the various exhibits. I wanted the objects to speak for themselves. I tried not to dramatize them in an over-the-top décor but to display them in an honest state of nakedness.

How does your show reflect the current mood?
Design is trying to get closer to art, to behave and function like art. That's because, basically, we've got enough of everything. What is really missing – and what will always be missing – is the poetry of being, the moment, the space, the object. The research we've done on the body is unique and poetical. It resists mass-production. Times of crisis are always favourable periods for creation and design.

People dare to change the codes and overthrow ideas.

But would you want to live with such objects?
Would you want to live with Rembrandt's *Slaughtered Ox*, a painting by Francis Bacon or a photo by Nan Golding? Like works of art, these objects have a strong personality and cannot be easily assimilated.

How did people react to the show?
Some were very interested, and others seemed slightly agitated.

What about the sex toys?
Funnily enough, no one mentioned them.

——

croisments.com

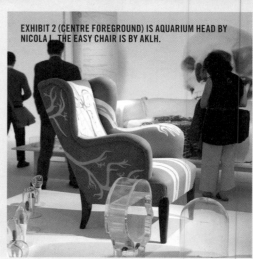

EXHIBIT 2 (CENTRE FOREGROUND) IS AQUARIUM HEAD BY NICOLA L. THE EASY CHAIR IS BY AKLH.

THE GESTURING HANDS (FOR HANGING UP YOUR COAT, IF YOU DARE) ARE BY THELERMONT HUPTON.

8

THIS PIECE FROM SAKAYA YAMAMOTO'S SKIN SERIES (SEEN ON SOFA) DEPICTS HOW A HIDE THROW WOULD LOOK IF MADE FROM HUMAN SKIN: IN THIS CASE, WITH FULL-BODY TATTOOS.

'I wanted to display these objects in an honest state of nakedness'
FRANÇOIS BERNARD

MAISON & OBJET

TYPE OF EVENT Professional trade show
LOCATION Paris
PRODUCT SECTOR Industrial and interior design
NUMBER OF EXHIBITORS 3000
NUMBER OF VISITORS 68,592
TARGET GROUP Design professionals and the general public
DURATION 4 – 8 September
FREQUENCY Biannually
WEBSITE EVENT maison-objet.com

OLE JENSEN'S HOT WATER BOTTLES (FOREGROUND) RESEMBLE HUMAN ORGANS.

PURAVIDA

A feminine aura surrounds the PuraVida collection. Curvaceously sloping sides flank the drain of the shallow, rounded washbasin, which is framed by a delicate rim. The basin is available in two sizes, with or without a supporting column or pedestal.

Duravit
duravit.com

FLOWING MAUVES

CERSAIE

The keywords at CERSAIE were space and serenity, as exemplified by fluidly formed washbasins and tiles in many shades of purple.

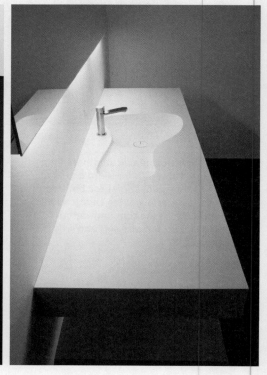

FARAWAY SQUARE
BY LUDOVICA AND ROBERTO PALOMBA

Designed by Ludovica and Roberto Palomba, the Faraway Square washbasin is part of a new bathroom collection by Kos. Characterized by its spare geometry, the basin is available as a floor- or wall-mounted model.
Dimensions: 95 x 56 x 88 cm.

Kos
kositalia.com

MINIWASH

Miniwash by Flaminia lives up to its name: the pieces of this bathroom collection are smaller than conventional sanitary appliances. Rounded corners soften the washbasin's basically angular form. The thickness of the ceramic has been kept to an absolute minimum.

Flaminia
ceramicaflaminia.it

FEET

Antonio Lupi's new Corian washbasin was created in collaboration with Nevio Tellatin. Characterizing the design is the contrast between the austere linearity of the volume containing the basin and the organic form of the basin itself. The Corian is 125 mm thick.

Antonio Lupi
antoniolupi.it

CERSAIE

TYPE OF EVENT Trade fair
LOCATION Bologna
PRODUCT SECTOR Ceramic tiles and bathroom furnishings
NUMBER OF EXHIBITORS 1036
NUMBER OF VISITORS 83,137
TARGET GROUP Trade professionals
DURATION 29 September – 3 October
FREQUENCY Annually
WEBSITE EVENT cersaie.it

NEW ZERO+

The latest interpretation of Catalano's Zero+ is the New Zero+, a sculptural collection that combines voluminous forms with finely crafted details. Accessories for the washbasin include a towel rail and a cabinet.

Catalano
catalano.it

HI-LINE

The name Hi-Line communicates more than one message. 'Hi' stands for Hidra and High: the brand and the quality of these bathroom furnishings. 'Line' refers to the characteristics of the products, which the company describes as 'fast and dynamic, but also soft and creamy'.

Hidra
hidra.it

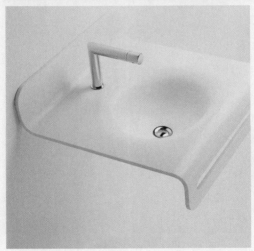

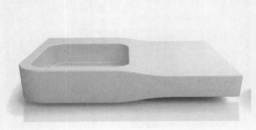

SHUI

An angular washbasin belonging to Ceramica Cielo's Shui collection: sanitaryware characterized by large volumes and striking proportions. Available in white, black and dark-grey and in the following three sizes: 80 x 48 x 15, 66 x 48 x 15 and 52 x 48 x 15cm.

Ceramica Cielo
ceramicacielo.it

WAVE
BY SIMONE MICHELI

Simone Micheli's Wave collection for Planit is made from white Corian. Washbasins are available (on request) with or without a hole for a mixer tap. A mirror accompanies Wave 4. Four models in various sizes.

Planit
planit.it

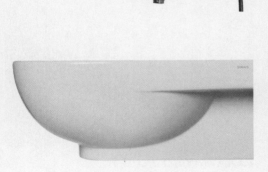

E-LINE BY TERRI PECORA

E-line is an Italian series of products produced by Simas and tailor made to suit the space in question. The collection is an example of strong, taut, organic design. Dimensions: 65 cm (basin with columnar support); 65 or 90 cm (wall-mounted models).

Simas
Simas.it

DÉCHIRER
BY PATRICIA URQUIOLA

Patricia Urquiola has created a range of oversize textured tiles for Mutina. Made from unglazed porcelain stoneware, the Déchirer collection features bas-relief patterns that add an intriguing play of light and shadow to the interior.
Mutina
mutina.it

MUST

An eco-friendly ceramic floor tile – a product by Novabell – Must comes in five colours and three sizes, and is also available as a brick-type mosaic. The material used contains 40% recycled material.
Novabell
novabell.it

DOUCE FRANCE
BY FABRIZIO ZANFI

The designer's perception of his beloved land, France, has been captured in this 31.5-x-31.5-cm floor tile. The simple design, traditional glaze and flecked surface reflect his roots. Available in the colours zinc, lead, nickel and lilac (shown here).
Viva
cerviva.it

BELLINI

Suitable for both traditional and contemporary interiors, Bellini is available in four colours: cream, copper, light green and pink. The gleaming surface of the 15-x-30-cm tile is the result of what the manufacturer calls a 'micro-relief' technique.
Kalebodur
kale.com.tr

CHÉRI

Technology and tradition go together in Chéri, a collection of ceramic tiles in soft, trendy colours, including the shade of purple shown here. Edilcuoghi's new line gives users a wide array of choices and a great opportunity for transforming any space into a place with a personal style.
Edilcuoghi
edilcuoghi.it

VETRINA

Vetrina is a collection of glass mosaic tiles remarkable for the broad range of colours available, a palette based on the Pantone system. Used creatively, the 10-x-10-mm tiles can produce everything from shaded effects and subtle nuances to vividly patterned surfaces. Vetrina includes 72 glossy and 32 matte shades, as well as 14 blends.
Mosaico
mosaicoitaliano.com

PANARA

A custom-made product line developed by
the design division of FMG, Panara is a collection
of floor tiles intended for outdoor use.
Colours: beige, black and taupe.

FMG
irisfmg.com

QUARZITES
BY PETRA AETERNA

An important feature of the new Petra Aeterna
collection is an anti-slip surface. These tiles are
suitable for indoor and outdoor applications
and for residential and office environments.
Quarzites are available in four colours: Silver,
Dorada, Alpes and Dark.

Iris
irisceramica.com

WAVE

The undulating effect produced by Fiandre's
Wave tiles is accentuated by a sober palette of
neutral colours: the tiles come in black, white and
grey and in three dimensions: 150 x 75, 75 x 75
and 75 x 37.5 cm.

Fiandre
granitifiandre.com

TRÈS JOLIE

Lea's new wall tiles are both colourful and
decorative. The Très Jolie collection comprises
four models, each with a distinctive style.
The tiles are available in four sizes. Three
complementary patterns complete the picture.

Lea
ceramichelea.it

TRACCE

Past and present, tradition and innovation,
history and breaking news: the themes on which
Refin based its Tracce tiles. Available in six
colours and three sizes, Tracce was designed
to facilitate installation.

Refin
refin.it

FUTURA

Diamonds provided the inspiration for Fap's
new collection of ceramic tiles, which are an
amalgamation of traditional, decorative
and contemporary design. Futura is available
in ten colours and in a mosaic mix.
Dimensions: 30.5 x 30.5 cm.

Fap
fapceramiche.com

EXINT

Highlighting a new outdoor collection by Mirage
are an interestingly textured surface and
five natural colours: Quotidien, Page, Fanon,
Noix and Tuile. It's a palette that offers users
an excellent opportunity to mix and match.
Dimensions: 30 x 60, 30 x 30 and 20 x 20 cm.

Mirage
mirage.it

PACE MAKER

Curator TULGA BEYERLE turned her attention to that most neglected aspect of the design profession – the daily grind – by following the schedules of seven design offices worldwide for Experimenta's Pace of Design exhibition.

WORDS **JANE SZITA**
PHOTOS **P EVOLUTION PRODUCTION**

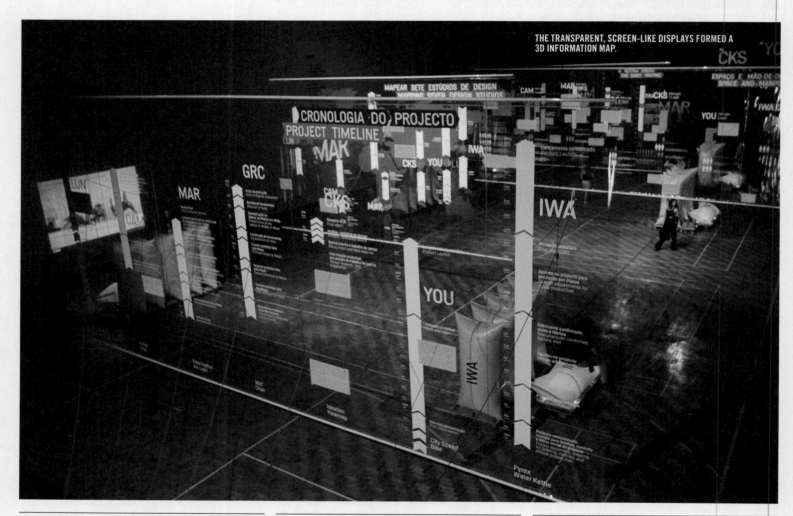

THE TRANSPARENT, SCREEN-LIKE DISPLAYS FORMED A 3D INFORMATION MAP.

This is very much an infographics show.
It is, because we wanted to focus on data and make it as visually accessible as possible. We didn't want the audience to have to read too much text.

How did you select the seven design studios in the study?
We wanted to look at cultural differences in the perception of time, so we picked studios that are representative of the local culture. The USA is known for its big industrial agencies, so we chose Lunar Design in San Francisco. In Japan we selected Ichiro Iwasaki – a large industrial office that's typical in that it works only for the Japanese market. Europe was perhaps the hardest, but we think that Konstantin Grcic, in Munich, best represents the intellectual quality that typifies Europe.

How did you gather the data?
We visited each office for two days with a photographer and just watched people. The photos of the whole day were condensed into 15-minute films and projected at the exhibition.

Explain how the show works.
First you see objects from each of the seven offices. Then you see how long it took to make each one – two years in the case of Lunar's toothbrush, for example. You also get to see where the studio is based and something about the daily routine – what they do for lunch, whether they work overtime and so forth. And you find out that Japanese designers work the longest hours and that Grcic has the most fixed working times.

What was your mission?
I wanted to demystify the idea of the designer as some sort of hero, and I wanted to tell a different story, rather than just putting an object on a pedestal. I wanted to tell normal people, who might not know about the design industry, the story behind creativity. It's hard work, and it's teamwork – not some lone genius coming up with ideas on his own. Designers are not the only ones involved in the process. Above all, it takes time.

What did you find most striking: the differences between the offices or the similarities?
There were more similarities than differences, although one factor that emerged strongly was that offices in Brazil,

EXPERIMENTADESIGN (EXD'09)

TYPE OF EVENT Design, architecture and creativity biennale
LOCATION Lisbon
NUMBER OF EVENTS 77
NUMBER OF VISITORS 120,000
TARGET GROUP Cultural and creative agents; students; academics; opinion makers and critics; politicians; mid- and high-level management officials from companies and institutions; journalists; general public
DURATION 9 September – 8 November
FREQUENCY Biannually
WEBSITE EVENT experimentadesign.pt

THE VARIOUS LAYERS OF INFORMATION USED THE METAPHOR OF THE SCREEN.

India and South Africa can afford the kind of staff that's beyond the means of European or North American offices. They have cooks and chauffeurs. Otherwise, the variation is in things like temperature and noise. Globalism makes transfer and connections easy and fast. But daily routine depends on expectations – the transport system, the local work ethic and so on. Wherever they are, designers tend to organize their schedules around the major local design fair.

What is the conclusion of Pace of Design, do you think?

One is certainly that, in creative work, the idea is the biggest challenge – but it's not the whole story. ▬▬

THE INTRODUCTION TO THE WORK OF INDIAN DESIGN AGENCY CKS; THE PROJECTED IMAGE ON THE WALL SHOWS THE COMPANY DIRECTOR, ADITYA DEV SOOD.

THE WAXMAN COMETH

EXPERIMENTADESIGN

JERSZY SEYMOUR's blood-red, poured-wax installation,
Open Source Amateur Diagram, invited visitors
to ExperimentaDesign Lisbon to add their own contributions
using sharpened bones.

WORDS **JANE SZITA**

How did Open Source Amateur Diagram work?
First we melted about 60 kg of blood-red
wax. We then poured it out to form an area
of about 3 x 3 m, which we etched with
sharpened bones – the most primeval of
tools – to inscribe the basis of the diagram
and to set out the idea of an 'amateur', non-
market-driven society. We invited people
to add and change things, which they did
– interestingly, in an almost childlike way.
We used soft wax, so it remained malleable.
It looks like art, but you call it design, don't you?
It's quite specifically design as far as I'm
concerned, because it asks what design's
position is now that its old mandate –

cheap products for the masses – is no more.
For some years now, I've been searching
for a kind of zero context for design, from
which to create participatory, situation-
driven work.
When, and why, did you start working with wax?
The idea of wax came from our research
into biodegradable materials for our Living
Systems project. The polycaprolactone
wax we use for the Amateur projects can
be melted down again and again. It is a
changeable, transformable material for
changeable, transformable desires. ▬
jerszyseymour.com

**JERSZY SEYMOUR
DESIGN WORKSHOP**

Jerszy Seymour was born in Canada and grew
up in London, where he studied industrial
design at the Royal College of Art. He began
his experimental and conceptual projects and
installations while living in Milan. Seymour has
also designed for companies like Magis, Vitra,
Kreo, Moulinex, SFR and IDEE. He has taught
widely and currently holds a guest professorship
at the HBK Saar. He lives and works in Berlin.

CHAIR MAN

EXPERIMENTADESIGN

Featured in MARCO SOUSA SANTOS' Workstation exhibition were 19 chairs that combine traditional assembly techniques with digital production methods.

WORDS **ROBERT THIEMANN**

In the late '90s, you were one of the cofounders of Proto Design, which was intended as a platform for launching Portuguese design. What happened to Proto?
We closed Proto when we realized that our main goal was to design and not to do business. We were tired of selling lamps. But we had lots of fun editing and presenting projects based on 'one material, one technology, and many designers'. We were partying all the time. Now I'm a teacher and a full-time designer collaborating mostly with Portuguese companies. Portugal has highly skilled manufacturers who are starting to understand the importance of a well-designed product and an effective communication strategy.

Why did you call your ExperimentaDesign presentation Workstation?
Workstation defines the period and the working environment in which I lived while doing this project. It's a kind of virtual working system involving people, technology, concepts and experiments – with one objective and for a certain period of time. It becomes a two-way dialectic process in which the designer is the trigger of a dynamic play of interaction with experts, their knowledge and technology.

You show no fewer than 19 chair designs. Do you have loads of energy, lots of time – or both?
It's something inherent to both designers and artists – and may be the only thing the two have in common – this natural addiction to creative action. For me, it's a need to experiment and try out materials. It's part of my nature, so it doesn't really require much energy; I just let myself go. But it's the results that excite me more than anything else and force me to keep going. When the developmental network is good, the results are quick and effective. Making this exhibition didn't take much time. Only eight months.

Why only chair designs? And what exactly are you researching?
The point of my research was to explore the possibilities of mixing traditional methods of assembly with a digital production process to make chairs. This isn't new, but it became the new paradigm of a design process in which digital production allows designers to be more independent of the industrial system. This paradigm has given designers flexibility and freedom, opening

new directions in style and, in many cases, blurring their focus and driving them towards decoration.
I wanted to get down to earth and to use these now-affordable production methods as part of a classical and rational approach to design. While exploring different chair typologies and considering certain design principles – such as lightness, structure, ergonomics and form – I've played with materials and developed a personal way of expressing the complexities involved in my research.

Will any of these designs be manufactured?
So far I have confirmation from two design editors, one in Portugal and one in Belgium, for distribution of eight of the 19 prototypes. I'll produce the other models myself and sell them to my regular clients.

You're one of the founders of ExperimentaDesign. How has the event

developed during the ten years of its existence?
At the beginning, we wanted to set up a platform in Lisbon for Portuguese designers to show their work to the international design community. As a peripheral country, we needed to direct attention to our design culture by organizing events with designers, producers and schools. But our biggest objective was to create a biennial cycle of 'experimental' presentations within the national design community. Now, ten years later, I'm glad that Experimenta still exists and that it's growing, but I'm sorry that the event hasn't shown the world the huge step taken by Portuguese designers and companies since we began our mission. Initially, Experimenta was committed to being a tool for the Portuguese design culture. Now it's something else. ▬▬▬

marcosousasantos.com

SIDEWAYS

EXPERIMENTADESIGN

MIGUEL VIEIRA BAPTISTA showed eight one-offs and limited-edition designs at Marz gallery – objects that explore the boundaries between ideas, prototypes and end products.

WORDS **ROBERT THIEMANN**

We rarely see you working outside Portugal nowadays. What does this say about the design scene?
It's true that I had many great opportunities during the late '90s. Until 2003, we developed a lot of projects in Lisbon that we showed abroad through Proto Design, the Portuguese Trade Institute and ExperimentaDesign. During those years I established good relationships with foreign manufacturers, but eventually these relationships and the industry changed. There were fewer and fewer investments and opportunities for showing Portuguese design at the right places in other countries. Currently, there are none at all.
The lack of commissions from Portuguese companies – who don't invest in product development – eventually pushed me into the gallery logic. This is not the kind of trendy thing that started some years ago in Paris and other European cities. It's a true opportunity for developing new projects in an atmosphere of total freedom, totally unrelated to corporate commissions. The gallery programme and the clients involved

are quite different from what you find in a traditional shop, so it's a perfect place for experimentation and intellectual debate. The art scene in Portugal is well developed, and design can profit from this well-organized, internationally active world.
Some of the designs you show at Marz gallery are made of paper, including renderings of tableware. Will they eventually be manufactured?
No, this is the actual project. The table set, Porcelana & Cortiça, explores the boundary between idea and product. Views from the side and above are printed on the outside of a cardboard box. This combination of technical drawing, presentation drawing and model gives the illusion of a real piece of porcelain. I found it very interesting to present finished pieces that 'talk' about the design process, especially the part that involves drawing as a tool. When you present cardboard pieces as finished objects, viewers might value the design process more than they do when seeing a traditional product made of porcelain. Of course, I would like to see these pieces

go into production, but that's another story.
What do you hope the Marz exhibition will bring you?
The possibility of doing other projects. It often happens that one thing leads to another.
What does ExperimentaDesign mean for the Portuguese design scene?
I think the opening week is tremendously impressive – loads of exhibition openings located in great buildings and lots of conferences with great speakers. After that, the energy you feel in the air starts to fade and eventually subsides to its normal level. ∎
mvbfactory.com

WATER BOMB

EXPERIMENTADESIGN

Design outfit Pedrita – RITA JOÃO and PEDRO FERREIRA – introduced a water bottle that looks like a cross between a hand grenade and a diamond.

WORDS **ROBERT THIEMANN**

Who initiated the project?
The project was born at our studio. It presented a challenge involving the space used for transport and for display at potential selling points. After we presented the project to Luso – Portugal's top water brand – we worked with their team to make the design feasible for production. We chose Luso because of the super quality of their water. Even though they don't have a so-called 'premium label,' their water tastes much better than a lot of other premium brands.

At the exhibition, you asked for feedback on the bottle design. What kind of response did you get?
People constantly asked where and when they can buy the product. Feedback has been very good. Catering companies seem to be very open to the project, particularly because it complements various table arrangements.

What does Luso think of the design?
Luso has been very interested in the design since the beginning. They're happy with the feedback and are looking at ways to launch the product.

Do you think the bottle will be manufactured?
Luso is evaluating the investment needed to optimize production and is studying possible target groups to prove its commercial value.

As participants in two main events and four side events, you've been quite involved in ExperimentaDesign. Does the Portuguese design scene benefit from this event?
It's a good event. It's the right size, and it makes an effort to show visitors new designs specific to the occasion. All of which means it's very important to the Portuguese design scene internally and externally. ExperimentaDesign is also a major social programme that supports a wider interchange of ideas and experiments. Currently, it's aiming for results directly related to greater advantages for Lisbon. ∎

pedrita.net

TIMBER!

NEUE RÄUME 09

Wood was everywhere at the NEUE RÄUME 09 fair, frequently looking as subtly charming as the event itself – as in this selection by Swiss designers.

FOGLIE SIDEBOARD

The horizontal stratification of this solid-wood sideboard is more than just an aesthetic addition to a functional object. The slender louvres are also used as 'handles' to open and close the drawers. Foglie features mortise and tenon joints. Drawers are available in different 'heights'. Suitable as a freestanding object or as a piece of furniture for use against a wall.

nut+grat
nutundgrat.ch

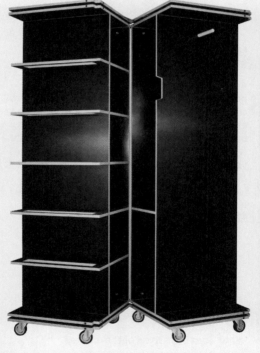

CHERRY TREE FROM MALANS
BY THOMAS LÖFFEL

A tower of blocks made from the wood of a cherry tree that grew in Malans, Switzerland, is the creation of Thomas Löffel, who used a chain saw to implement the design – or is it a work of art? In any case, it provides an interesting set of shelves for books or other items worthy of display.

Spoon
thomas-spoon.ch

TURNABLE
BY SEBASTIAN DÄSCHLE

A revolving wardrobe provides storage for clothes, a mirror for reflection and casters for mobility. What designer Sebastian Däschle calls 'an endless hinge' allows the wardrobe to be opened from all sides. The material is quality plywood. Turnable measures 185 x 110 x 55 cm.

Dua
dua-collection.com

GHOST

Part of Mint's Living Room range of furniture, Ghost is a chair finished in wood veneer. The concept of the collection is a domestic environment that breathes. A close relative of Ghost is Air – nearly identical, but Air has a coloured plastic seat.

Mint
mintfurniture.lv

SPLER
BY RAMON ZANGGER

Spler – the word for 'butterfly' in one of Switzerland's Romansch dialects – is the work of Ramon Zangger, who has designed two differently decorated models, both made from cedar. The theme of the cabinet pictured here is Switzerland's trilingual status. The front of the piece is covered with the words 'Italiano', 'Deutsch' and 'Français.'

ramonzangger.ch

SABOOH
BY ANNA BLATTERT AND DANIEL GAFNER

Underpinning Anna Blattert and Daniel Gafner's Sabooh lamp is energy-saving LED technology combined with the designers' impression of Oriental lanterns. The rather twiggy, angular frame of the floor lamp – made from sustainable oak – features an outstretched arm that keeps the lampshade poised above the surface most in need of light.

Postfossil
postfossil.ch

NAN15 BOOKSHELVES
BY NITZAN COHEN

An ingenious design by Nitzan Cohen, Nan15's base and back form a module. Multiple modules can be assembled to build a structure of virtually any size. The product has a slightly inclined base and, on either end, side walls positioned at right angles. The result is a shelving system on which you can display your books and rest assured that they will remain in position, even when one is removed.

Nanoo
nanoo.ch

ONO
BY MATTHIAS WEBER

With more to offer than simply a dynamic, timeless quality, this lightweight stacking chair by Matthias Weber feels equally at home in a private setting or a public space. Highlight is a pair of broad armrests. Available in solid beech, oak and American walnut. Optional cushions add a lovely layer of comfort.

Dietiker Switzerland
dietiker.com

NEUE RÄUME 09

TYPE OF EVENT International home furniture fair
LOCATION Zurich
PRODUCT SECTOR Furniture, textiles, lighting, floor and wall coverings, kitchen and bathroom furnishings
NUMBER OF EXHIBITORS 90
NUMBER OF VISITORS 30,000
TARGET GROUP Consumers, designers, architects and interior designers
DURATION 24 October – 1 November
FREQUENCY Annually
WEBSITE EVENT neueraeume.ch

PRIMAVERA
BY JÖRG BONER

Jörg Boner has designed a highly functional collection of outdoor furniture for Tossa. The solid-wood pieces are made from various kinds of weather-resistant timber and have bases of fibre-reinforced concrete. Dimensions: table 83 x 92 x 72 cm; bench 39 x 45 cm.

Tossa
tossa.ch

DAVE N. PORT
BY ROLF CARL NIMMRICHTER

Designed by Rolf Carl Nimmrichter for Aer, Dave N. Port is a small desk for bedroom or study, measuring a mere 29 x 31.5 x 23.5 cm. Made from certified timber – walnut and oak – the desk has one leather-clad section, one wooden section and a sliding mechanism that opens the desk to reveal a storage compartment. Wiring is concealed in the legs.

Aer
aer.ch

COLLEGE MATERIAL

STUDENTS claimed centre stage at Dutch Design Week, where we found a strong focus on raw, natural and unusual materials.

**RAW TABLE WARE
BY JOCHEM DE WIT**

1985, the Netherlands
ArtEZ Art & Design, Arnhem
Product Design
jochemdewit.nl

The unusual materials that Jochem de Wit chose for his products include enamelled concrete, for soup bowls; beech veneer, for spoons; bronze, for egg cups; and brick, for jugs and cups. These are not clean, pristine, austerely designed objects but a range of items with unique personalities. De Wit's Raw Table Ware has already been added to The Frozen Fountain collection (frozenfountain.nl).

PHOTO **MICHEL VAN DE WIEL**

REINVENTING THE VIDEO TAPE
BY AISHA IFITIKHAR

1987, United Kingdom
Central Saint Martins, London
Textile Design
aisha@mywebspace.co.uk

Aisha Ifitikhar is breathing new life into nearly
extinct videotape. She subjects videotape to a
number of techniques before weaving the strands
to make what appear to be fabrics. Her varied
collection is the result of the diversity of methods
she applies to the tape, which generate an array
of structures, textures and surfaces. Reinventing
the Video Tape is suitable for countless
applications.

PHOTO **LISA KLAPPE**

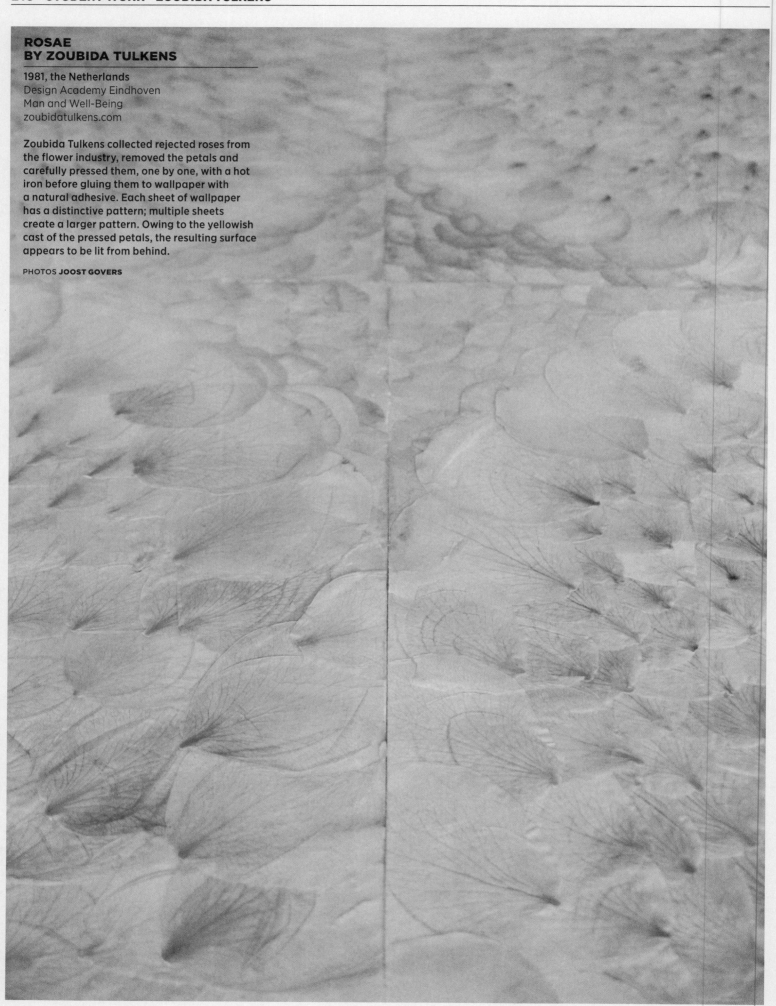

**ROSAE
BY ZOUBIDA TULKENS**

1981, the Netherlands
Design Academy Eindhoven
Man and Well-Being
zoubidatulkens.com

Zoubida Tulkens collected rejected roses from
the flower industry, removed the petals and
carefully pressed them, one by one, with a hot
iron before gluing them to wallpaper with
a natural adhesive. Each sheet of wallpaper
has a distinctive pattern; multiple sheets
create a larger pattern. Owing to the yellowish
cast of the pressed petals, the resulting surface
appears to be lit from behind.

PHOTOS **JOOST GOVERS**

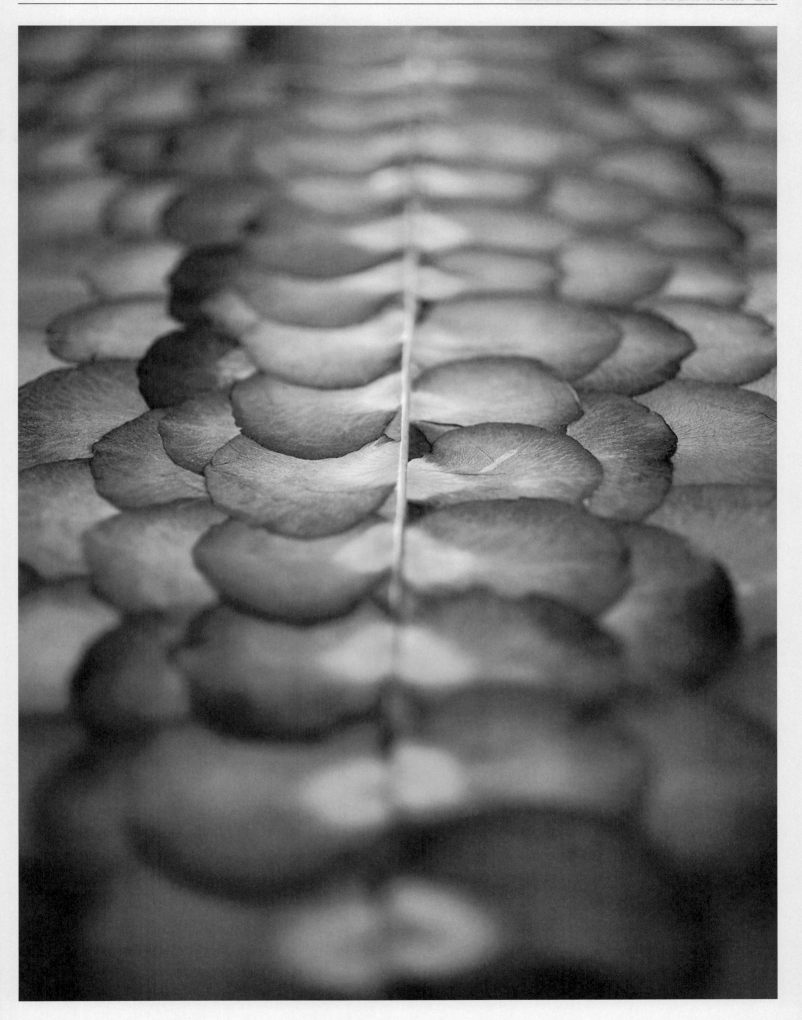

INK STORM
BY MARK VAN GENNIP

1979, the Netherlands
Design Academy Eindhoven
Man and Identity
mrrk.nl

An experiment by Mark van Gennip began by
pouring water over fabric whose dyes had not
been fixed. Some of the cloth was left out in the
rain, and some was doused by hand. The process
resulted in what Van Gennip calls 'an ink storm',
during which the dyed patterns transformed
from static geometric designs into dramatic
organic motifs. Each 'storm' created unexpected
chromatic nuances and new forms, resulting in
a beautiful collection of silk fabrics suitable for
the fashion industry.

PHOTOS **CATH HERMANS**

TEXTILE MADE FRAGILE
BY DJIM BERGER

1980, the Netherlands
Design Academy Eindhoven
Man and Well-Being
djimberger.com

After pulling woollen yarns through coloured clay, Djim Berger 'wove' them to produce a gossamer-thin blanket. While the cloth was being fired in the kiln, the yarn disintegrated, leaving only a porcelain object marked by the textured pattern of the yarn. During a second firing, at a higher temperature, three metal supports gave Textile Made Fragile its draped form. The object can support only lightweight accessories.

PHOTOS RENE VAN DER HULST

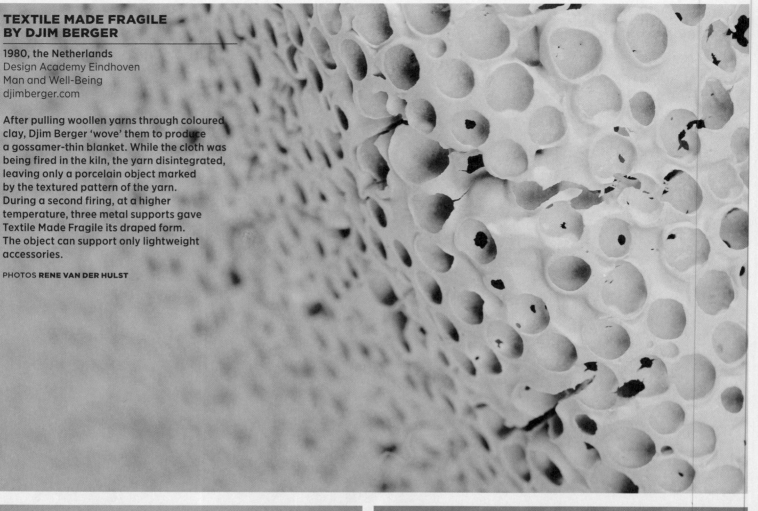

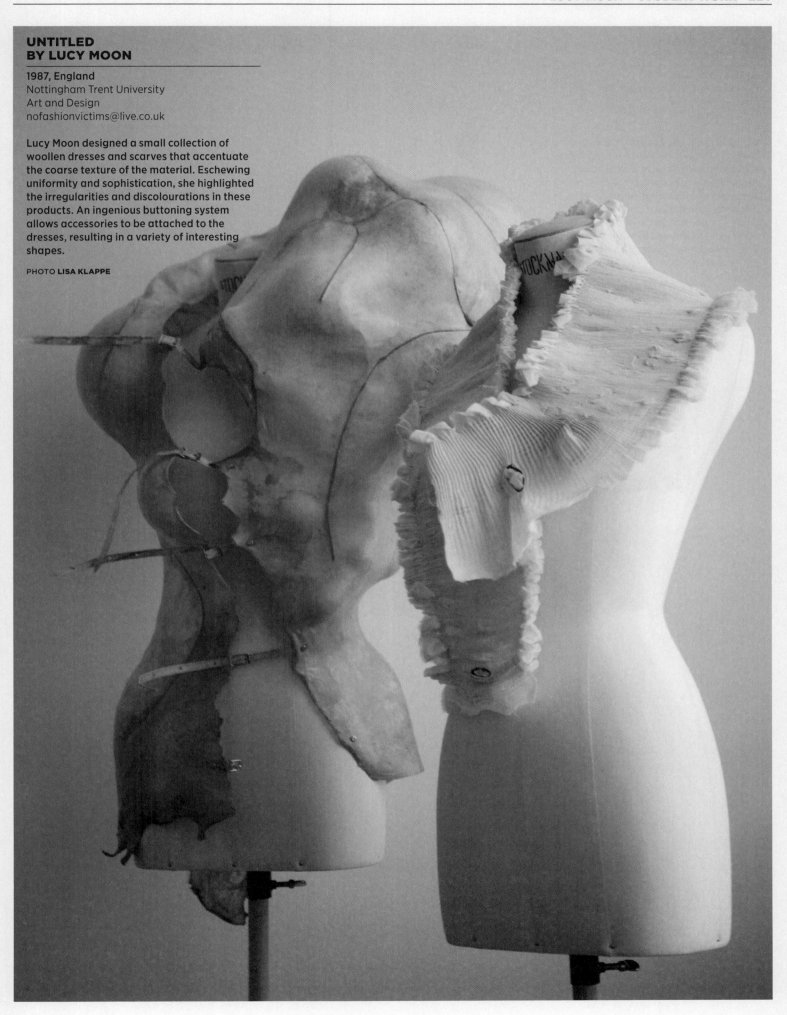

UNTITLED
BY LUCY MOON

1987, England
Nottingham Trent University
Art and Design
nofashionvictims@live.co.uk

Lucy Moon designed a small collection of woollen dresses and scarves that accentuate the coarse texture of the material. Eschewing uniformity and sophistication, she highlighted the irregularities and discolourations in these products. An ingenious buttoning system allows accessories to be attached to the dresses, resulting in a variety of interesting shapes.

PHOTO **LISA KLAPPE**

FOR THE BIRDS
BY FLORIAN KRÄUTLI

1985, Switzerland
Design Academy Eindhoven
Man and Living
kraeutli.com

These lampshades are made from ground beet
roots, cabbages, leeks, tapioca and wafers.
You can alter the function of the objects by
using them outdoors, thus shifting them from
the private to the public domain. When they
are hung from the branches of trees, they
become tasty snacks for birds and other
animals. Outdoor use represents an irreversible
process, however; eventually, nothing remains
of For the Birds.

PHOTO **VINCENT VAN GURP**

PAPERPULP CABINETS
BY DEBBIE WIJSKAMP

1984, the Netherlands
ArtEZ Art & Design Arnhem
Product Design
debbiewijskamp.com

To develop a new building material made from
discarded items, Debbie Wijskamp began by
researching ways in which to reuse old (news)
paper. She combined pulp and a bonding agent
to make sturdy building blocks, from which
she constructed handsome cabinets. The new
material can be used in various ways and is
suitable for all sorts of products.

PHOTO **LISA KLAPPE**

DUTCH DESIGN WEEK

TYPE OF EVENT Design festival
LOCATION Eindhoven
PRODUCT SECTOR Industrial, conceptual, spatial, graphic
and food design; textiles and fashion; design management;
trendspotting
NUMBER OF SUB-EVENTS 290
NUMBER OF VISITORS 115,000 (up from 80,000 in 2008)
TARGET GROUP Designers, manufacturers
and educational institutions
DURATION 17 – 25 October
FREQUENCY Annually
WEBSITE EVENT dutchdesignweek.nl

MONEY PIG
BY ROBERT BRONWASSER

Each object in Robert Bronwasser's DSGN collection, produced and sold by Royal Goedewaagen, bears the distinctive signature of a man whose crisp shapes are invariably both decorative and functional. Money Pig – a ceramic piggy bank with a removable nose – measures 15 x 15 x 18 cm. Royal Goedewaagen, which has been in business for almost 400 years, is known for its quality, handcrafted products.

Smool
smool.nl

DUTCH DOMESTICITY
WOONBEURS

In Amsterdam, design talents presented their latest products: a combination of traditional Dutch detail and exciting innovation.

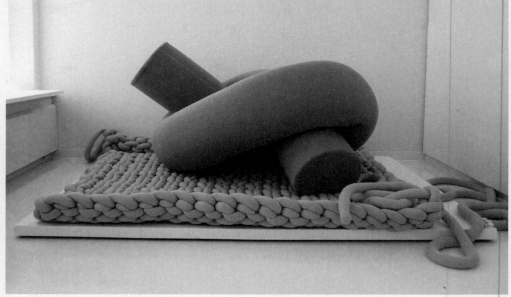

STONESTOVE
BY DICK VAN HOFF

Weltevree is a Dutch brand that develops and manufactures authentic products for the domestic environment – appliances that satisfy our basic desires. Weltevree stands for distinction, originality and excellence. Shown here is Dick van Hoff's Stonestove, a classic from 1999 that is only now available on the consumer market.

Weltevree
weltevree.info

PHAT KNITS
BY BAUKE KNOTTNERUS

A collection of supersize furniture created by Dutch designer Bauke Knottnerus, Phat Knit features items that are actually crafted on giant knitting needles. One piece features thick coils of 'yarn' that can be tied or woven together, while another consists of a single giant knot. Knottnerus knits a range of furnishings, including rugs and various types of seating.

baukeknottnerus.nl

WOONBEURS

TYPE OF EVENT Home and lifestyle fair for consumers and professionals
LOCATION Amsterdam
NUMBER OF EXHIBITORS 300
NUMBER OF VISITORS 80,000 visitors, 5,000 professionals
TARGET GROUP Consumers, architects, stylists, retailers, designers, buyers
DURATION 26 September – 4 October
FREQUENCY Annually
WEBSITE EVENT woonbeurs.nl

PORCELAIN WALLPAPER
BY STUDIO DITTE

The result of rummaging through china cabinets and browsing around antique markets, Studio Ditte's Porcelain Wallpaper offers a pretty pattern of dishes that is perfect for a cosy dining area or for that special corner of the house reserved for a cup of tea and a moment of relaxation. Length: 6 m. Pattern repeat: 3 m.

studioditte.nl

BLOW AWAY VASE
BY FRONT

Front digitized a Royal Delft vase with the use of 3D software, changed the parameters and exposed the object to a simulated gust of wind. Recently acquired by the Victoria and Albert in London, the Blow Away Vase is part of the museum's permanent collection.

Moooi
moooi.com

KNICK KNACK
BY KIKI VAN EIJK

Drawing inspiration from typical Japanese-made bowls and cups, Kiki van Eijk crafted a series of pots featuring bas-relief patterns that include the outlines of what she calls 'everyday knick-knacks'. The pots come in two patterns and four colours: black, white, mint green and KLM blue. Used alone or in multiples, Knick Knack enhances nearly any environment.

kikiworld.nl

CABINET
BY CHRIS SLUTTER

Chris Slutter's brand-new design, Cabinet, was unveiled at the Home Furniture Fair in Amsterdam. Underlining the cabinet's clean lines and simple form is the use of traditional colours: cool white or warm brown. Slanted doors are emphasized by Cabinet's perfectly rectangular sides. Photo Arjan Benning.

chrisslutter.nl

FAÇADE WALLPAPER
BY MUURBLOEM

Traditional styles and techniques are a source of motivation for Muurbloem, whose designers specialize in interior products such as furniture and wall coverings. Working with clients to create the desired effect, they produce spaces imbued with both intimacy and surprise. Shown here is Muurbloem's wallpaper design for Korein, a large day nursery in Eindhoven, the Netherlands.

muurbloem.com

MATTER CITY AND MATTER HOUSE
BY TAS-KA

Dutch designers Hester Worst and Jantien Baas of Tas-Ka created Matter City and Matter House, which can be used as pillows, as interior accessories or as toys for building a miniature town in the playroom or bedroom, for example. The inner cushion is a combination of foam rubber and fibrefill, but each item is custom-made according to the buyer's choice of fabric and colourway.

tas-ka.nl

MOOD SWINGS

The unique quality and high aspirations of MOOD BRUSSELS prove what can happen when a trade fair features only 'original designs'.

01
DESIGNO

This highly textured, stylish product offers an endless array of applications. Used as a wall covering, Designo unites the elegance and soft metallic sheen of patent leather with a futuristic 3D surface design. Patterns available include squares, rectangles, pyramids and circles. Comes in various densities and hardnesses.

Hulshof Royal Dutch Tanneries
hulshof.com

02
49570

Upholstery fabric 49570 belongs to Baumann Dekor's modern-design collection. Based on the image of a wave, the fabric creates a three-dimensional effect that enhances virtually any interior.

Baumann Dekor
baumann.co.at

03
TEX-TREME COLLECTION

Spun, woven and finished by means of a special technique, this outdoor fabric has a textured, waffle-like surface that is weather-, insect- and fade-resistant. Made from an eco-friendly fibre, the UV-absorbent Tex-Treme fabrics are the result of a sustainable production process that reduces waste and uses no heavy metals or chemicals.

Gebr. Munzert
munzert.de

04
E-1715/ G ARABESQUE

Part of Naturtex's collection of embossed 'mirror fabrics', E-1715/ G Arabesque is available in 14 colours. An even greater range of shades – both shiny and matte – is produced when the product is embossed. The fabric is ideal as a covering for furniture, but it can also be used to clad MDF panels as a solution for walls or ceilings.

Naturtex
naturtex.es

MOOD BRUSSELS

TYPE OF EVENT International trade fair
LOCATION Brussels
PRODUCT SECTOR Window, wall and furniture coverings.
NUMBER OF EXHIBITORS 290
NUMBER OF VISITORS 8,350
TARGET GROUP Wholesalers, furniture manufacturers and chain stores
DURATION 08 – 11 September
FREQUENCY Annually
WEBSITE EVENT moodbrussels.com

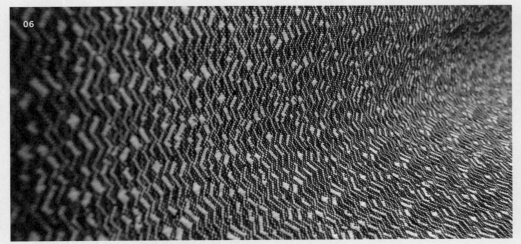

05
SKYSCRAPER

A look of exclusivity marks Deltracon's Skyscraper, a fabric used as a window covering. Made of 80% linen and 20% polyester, the product – clearly inspired by architecture – is a fusion of softness, luxury and modernity.

Deltracon
deltracon.be

06
ANGELI #16

The gleam emitted by this heavy polyester fabric – for use as an upholstery textile, as well as for panels and curtains – comes from Etun's clever combination of shiny black and coloured fibres. When exposed to natural light, Angeli #16 shimmers as if the entire spectrum were trapped inside the fabric.

Etun Ltd.

07
OUTDOOR-QUALITY UPHOLSTERY

Classy upholstery fabric for outdoor use, this eco-friendly, 100% recyclable product by Weverij Van Neder is non-allergenic and mould- and bacteria-resistant. It protects outdoor furniture from damage by saltwater, chlorine, acids, sunscreen, perspiration and stains. Above all, the fabric adapts to the temperature, warming you when it's cold and cooling you when it's hot.

Weverij van Neder
vanneder.be

08
CANE-BRAKE

Innovation in the form of a striking Jacquard weave, Cane-Brake features viscose raffia on a polyester yarn backing. The result is fascinating.

Fratelli Reali
fratellireali.it

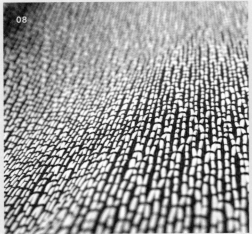
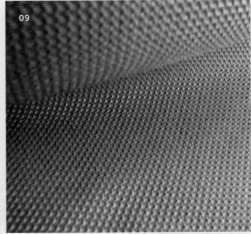

09
MESH

This attractively sbructured polyester wall covering – currently in the final stages of development – will be available in ten bright colours that reflect light and produce an intriguing effect.

Tietex International
tietex.com

SO YOUNG

VIENNA DESIGN WEEK

Shown outside Asia for the first time at Vienna Design Week,
MICHAEL YOUNG's Works in China are products
of his enthusiasm for industrial processes.

WORDS **JANE SZITA**
PHOTOS **COURTESY OF MICHAEL YOUNG**

CONSTRUCTED FROM MODULAR ALUMINIUM UNITS, THE ZIPTE LINK
INSTALLATION HAS GROWN ORGANICALLY TO BECOME A LARGE AND
PUZZLING FORM.

What inspired your Works in China series?
I started up the project five years ago. The aim was to design a range of unbranded products with Chinese factories. Since there was no branding, we could start afresh, creating processes and typologies my way, without any restraint. Now I'm helping all these companies build up their images and product ranges, so they can make the things I think are worth making.

You opened your studio in Hong Kong in 2006. Did you have a lot to learn about working in China?
I wouldn't like to do it all over again, quite honestly – arriving in Asia with a suitcase is about as nerve-racking as it gets. But I'm fortunate in that I have built things up slowly, and now I'm working with wonderful people and companies who have joy, passion and honesty and who believe in me. It's not like Europe, where we just hand over the design drawings and almost say goodbye. Here I have had to create a team for each step. My first project here was with a very old Chinese family that used to run the place before Mao took over, and sometimes I was out of my depth. I'm not one to keep my mouth shut: I've learned to be fearless, which is not something I expected to be a part of my job. I've also had to become good in business, as a designer is hopeless without that. Design is the smallest part of it at times – the important part is to understand how to work with Chinese company structures and to get to grips with the many layers involved, because there can be a lot of politics. But you can only learn these things by being thrown in at the deep end.

How do these Chinese pieces fit in with your other work?
I don't think they do fit. They are actually in contradiction to my other works, because with them I had total control all the way. These objects look how I wanted them to look. Neither of us is supposed to know this, but if you use a factory that designs products for Apple, and then take those skills outside the electronics framework to make a chair, you are really in a whole new world.

A new industrial world?
I'm drawn to the beauty of the machine. I'm not much into historical design at all. I love post-World War II products, designed at a time when engineers needed to make efficient products and to add aesthetics in a simple way. I love factories and processes. I'm not an artist. However, while I'm very much an industrial designer, I like the freedom that artists have. A fundamental issue for me is that when I was younger I didn't think the world was really a place I wanted to live in.

Why did you take this show to Vienna first, rather than to another European fair?
This may be an important body of work for me, but starting it in a major city didn't matter. I wanted to step into Europe slowly and to have the process grow organically. Vienna wasn't directly a sales mission for me, I would prefer to see it as a cultural event for people who enjoy design. The opening answered so many questions for so many people working in Europe. I take for granted production processes that Europe-based designers believe are rocket science. Vienna is a very useful event. I noticed that old companies are starting to work with young Austrian designers. I normally avoid design fairs, but I liked this one.

YOUNG INTENDS ZIPTE LINK TO BE SEEN NOT AS DESIGN ART, BUT AS INDUSTRIAL ART.

CARBON TABLE: THE SERIES ALSO FEATURES SPECIAL CARBON-FIBRE PIECES, LIKE THIS ONE.

A CARBON LIMITED-EDITION VERSION OF THE AWARD-WINNING COEN CHAIR FOR ACCUPUNTO.

ZIPTE LINK TABLE IN RED.

VIENNA DESIGN WEEK

TYPE OF EVENT Design festival
LOCATION Vienna
NUMBER OF EXHIBITORS The festival has 50 programme partners (museums, institutions, shops, galleries) and 46 designers were featured in the last edition
NUMBER OF VISITORS 19,000
TARGET GROUP People interested in design - especially designers, architects, culturally involved people, tourists, students, children
DURATION 1 – 11 October
FREQUENCY Annually
WEBSITE EVENT viennadesignweek.at

CHAIR4A, IN ALUMINIUM, IS DESCRIBED BY YOUNG AS 'A BREAKTHROUGH IN CHINA, A REAL PIECE OF CHINESE INDUSTRIAL MAGNIFICENCE – WITHOUT WANTING TO SOUND TOO BOLD'.

How did the Chinese reaction to your show vary from that of Vienna?

The reaction in Vienna was quite breathtaking. I met people from all walks of life, including students who got it straightaway and CEOs who wanted to buy it all. In China, design is taken for granted a little more, but it's getting better.

Do you approach industrial design, furniture and interiors differently?

I approach them all the same way. They're all the same to me. My interiors are full of the items I've created, so in that sense my interiors are quite industrial, which is how I want them.
They're made with materials of our times. I approach all things with an eye on the high-end mass market, but along the way I pause for the odd experiment, like the Carbon Coen or the birdhouse I made from folded paper.

Do you have a favourite piece in Works in China?

Well, Chair4A. It's a breakthrough in China, a real piece of Chinese industrial magnificence – without wanting to sound too bold.

You've lived abroad for a long time now. What are the creative consequences?

It's perfect. I don't need cultural influences. I'm my own man, but the nearer you are to a good factory the easier it is to play. I get to do things now that I couldn't do otherwise. Hong Kong is a hub for trading offices, and there's a lot going on. I have never looked for a project during my time here. It's all word of mouth, so one can get creative respect here, too. Living outside Europe is perfect. I'm a romantic adventurer. I love Europe, though – the hills, the food, the calm, the wine – but I'm pretty international. If I'm not in Hong Kong, I'm in Sydney. If I'm not there, I'll be in Tokyo or Bali or Shanghai – I move and live.

Should we still consider you an English designer?

Yes. It's in my DNA. I'm utterly English. I like Prince Charles, ropery, old telephones boxes – all that's important to me. As a designer you need to be globally minded, but changing location would be a very poor excuse for losing touch with who you are.

What piece of work most represents who you are as a designer?

Right now, the Cityspeed bike, for its details, form, processes, finishes.

Summarize your design philosophy, please.

Do what you want to do; just make it worthwhile for all involved.

Which designer do you admire most?

Phillipe Starck has created and is still creating some unquestionably amazing things.

What inspires you?

The interaction between materials and machines. Otherwise, I do what I do and always have. I just like machines that make things, and I like personal comfort – a healthy mix! I'm not a market-driven concept creator, but I do help a lot of large brands.

Has the credit crunch affected your work?

Only in a positive way. Factories needed to keep the machines pumping, which helped with the production for my show.

Your biggest remaining design ambition?

To redesign the Jaguar E-Type series.

■■■ michael-young.com

GLOBAL WITNESS

COPENHAGEN DESIGN WEEK

Rather than back-to-the-basics simplicity, Scandinavian companies took a good look at the world and displayed a cornucopia of colour at COPENHAGEN DESIGN WEEK.

PO_STACK
BY ANDERS BRIX

A shelving system marked by flexibility, variation and a sculptural look, po_stack was created by Anders Brix. Easy to assemble, the units can be stacked and arranged in countless ways. When the system is used as a room divider, the shelves (either open or closed) are accessible from both sides. Mix and match colours, reconfigure the entire arrangement, buy extra units to expand shelving space – the possibilities are limitless with po_stack.

PO2
po2.dk

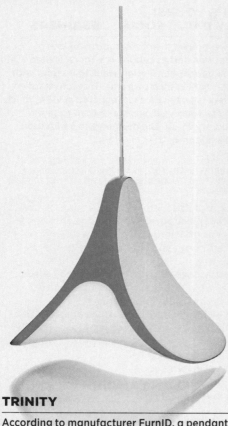

TRINITY

According to manufacturer FurnID, a pendant lamp designed in 2009 should look exactly like this one does. Trinity has three surfaces, thus its name. Although each of the lamp's two sides is unique, they create a harmonious whole and have the same function: to illuminate the surrounding space with a soft, warm glow. The third 'surface', at the bottom of the lamp, illuminates the desk or table below, producing light suitable for working or reading.

Furnid
furnid.com

NW1
BY NICHOLAI WIIG HANSEN

Plain, traditional, modern – and stunning. This sculptural table in stoneware is the brainchild of Danish designer Nicholai Wiig Hansen, who found his colours in the work of regional artists whose paintings are filled with the natural organic beauty and light of Scandinavia. NW1 is part of the Normann Copenhagen furniture line, which combines the ever-popular Danish Modern look with cutting-edge innovation. The table is suitable for both indoor and outdoor use.

Normann Copenhagen
normann-copenhagen.com

COAT TREE
BY SIDSE WERNER

Designed by the late Sidse Werner, Coat Tree has a light, fragile look that belies its reputation as a robust object strong enough to hold a surprising number of coats. Underlining the dynamic design is Coat Tree's ability to blend into its surroundings and thus complement the style of any interior. Coat Tree is available in powder-coated chromed steel and as a multicoloured, white or multi-grey model.

Fritz Hansen
fritzhansen.com

COPENHAGEN DESIGN WEEK

TYPE OF EVENT Design festival
LOCATION Copenhagen
PRODUCT SECTOR Furniture
NUMBER OF EXHIBITORS 500
NUMBER OF VISITORS Data not yet available
TARGET GROUP Professionals, manufacturers and everyone interested in design
DURATION 27 August - 6 September
FREQUENCY Under consideration (probably annually)
WEBSITE EVENT copenhagendesignweek.dk

GUBI CHAIR
BY KOMPLOT

The first industrial product based on an innovative German technique for moulding wood veneer is Gubi, a chair designed by Komplot. The Gubi collection features chairs and tables in three heights for restaurants, cafés, conference rooms, lounges, offices and home environments. Chairs come in four models and six sizes. Options include leather or fabric upholstery and a wide range of colours.

Gubi
gubi.dk

IT'S YOURS!
BY RACA, SOCIAL DESIGNERS

Questioning the contemporary values of a nation and its culture, It's Yours! invited visitors to Copenhagen Design Week to interact with Denmark in their own way. This conversation piece is based on a law enacted in 1854, which gives Danish citizens the right to raise the country's flag. The designers at RACA used silk paper for their creation.

raca.dk

MARIMEKKO COLLECTION

The latest breathtaking collection by Marimekko plays with cheery contrasts and warm colours reminiscent of summer. Marimekko, which has exhibited at the Gallery Fashion Fair in Copenhagen since 2007, treated visitors to Copenhagen Design Week to a fashion show. Look for Marimekko products next spring, when they will be on view in several of the world's leading design capitals.

Marimekko
marimekko.fi

ROOF

The roof as icon: it's this simple notion that led to Goodmorning Technology's Roof lamps, a collection of no-nonsense pendants, wall lamps, floor lamps and table lamps. Equipped with an intuitive sensor for dimming or intensifying light, Roof invites users to get involved in the decision-making process: romantic and cosy, brilliant and lively – or something in between? Lamps are made of painted aluminium.

Goodmorning Technology
gmtn.dk

MP MINI
BY PETER J. LASSEN
AND JOAKIM LASSEN

MP Mini – a series of café, coffee and lounge tables with round, square and oval tops – is the work of Peter J. Lassen and Joakim Lassen. Combining simplicity and functionality with an array of bright colours, MP Mini tables reflect Montana's aim to create unique spaces punctuated with personality. Available in 44 colours, MP Mini offers a table for every task.

Montana
montana.dk

KLÁRA ŠUMOVÁ'S SERVING TABLE AND A BREAD BASKET BY POLKA.

ALFREDO HÄBERLI'S CINDERELLA IN GLASS (CENTRE).

LOVE OBJECTS

DESIGNBLOK'09

While breathing new life into the Czech heritage crafts of ceramics and glass, Křehký's show at DESIGNBLOK'09 explored the home 'as a space for joy and happiness'.

WORDS **JANE SZITA**
PHOTOS **SALIM ISSA**

Combining contemporary design and the heritage traditions of Czech ceramics and glass, the Křehký (it means 'fragile') project's specially commissioned pieces – by the likes of Maxim Velčovský – formed the backbone of its successful Emotional Landscape of Contemporary Czech Design show, which opened at Designblok back in 2007. Two years on, with another crop of freshly commissioned pieces in the pipeline and another edition of Designblok to show them at, curators Jana Zielinksy and Jiří Macek decided to enter 'the inimate landscape of home', in Macek's words. But, much as the Emotional Landscape was inspired by the Narnia of C.S. Lewis, Zielinsky and Macek's home became 'the landscape of stories and magic'. Banal domesticity was banished by a 'slightly surreal' installation by the appropriately named Dáda Němeček, in which elaborately beautiful vases held dead flowers, and objects were heaped haphazardly together, some upside down or balancing on top of others. The well-lit and predominantly white or glass pieces, set against a deeply shadowed background relieved only by a projected window framing a luminous tree, seemed to glow from within. 'Home as a protected space is full of objects

that come to us so that we can fulfil our dreams of harmony,' says Jiří Macek. 'We define our notions of happiness through objects. The objects that visitors found at the Micro-World of Joy were created from the inner needs of the designers. The only theme that Jana Zielinski and I determined for the new edition of Křehký was home as a space for joy and happiness, a space in which we feel like ourselves.'
The wide brief, and a catholic selection of designers, led to an interesting variety of work, from the precise but poetic Cinderella glass creation (a game, apparently) by Alfredo Häberli, one of littala's favourite guest designers, to Natassia Aleinikava's Spider lamps, inspired by the traditional protective symbols used in homes in her native Belarus. Collectively, 'the result represents an intimate landscape in which we venture deeper below the surface of objects, to ourselves,' says Macek. 'It is a quest for miraculous moments in an ordinary day.'

DESIGNBLOK 09

TYPE OF EVENT Exhibition of contemporary Czech and international design
LOCATION Prague
PRODUCT SECTOR Industrial design, fashion, furniture, ceramics, glass and more
NUMBER OF EXHIBITORS 212
NUMBER OF VISITORS 35,000
TARGET GROUP Students, professionals, design buyers, talent scouts, manufacturers and the general public
DURATION 5 October - 11 October
FREQUENCY Annually
WEBSITE EVENT designblok.cz

IMAGERY'S NICEST TEDDY BEARS WITH CHILDREN'S CHAIRS BY OLGOJ CHORCHOJ.

THE EXHIBITION DESIGN, BY DÁDA NĚMEČEK, GAVE THE DOMESTIC
OBJECTS A SLIGHTLY SURREAL ATMOSPHERE.

IN THE KNOW

The authors of four new books let us in on the secrets of modular structures, communication technologies, the spatial use of graphics and contemporary trends in furniture design.

WORDS MILOU STEEGMAN

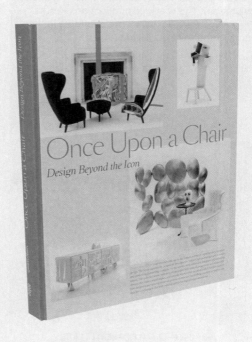

ONCE UPON A CHAIR
DESIGN BEYOND THE ICON

International and up-to-the minute, this predominantly visual survey of contemporary furniture design celebrates the current progressive, artisanal, and narrative trends in the discipline.

Once Upon a Chair – a detailed, international, mainly visual survey of current tendencies and developments in furniture and interior design – captures the *Zeitgeist* marking this rigorous field. The book features work by the world's most promising young designers and spots several key trends that indicate a recognizable shift towards progressive designs with the power to make a social impact. The photographs show ample evidence that the designer-meets-artisan phenomenon is reviving craftsmanship and elevating old traditions to new levels of luxury, and that today's conscious effort to produce sustainable design is benefitting from environmentally friendly materials and manufacturing methods developed to increase product durability. Along with information about the designers and their projects, the book illustrates ways in which process-driven, storytelling concepts – often implemented in a collage-like manner – are used to craft flexible furniture systems. *Once Upon a Chair* celebrates the unrestrained, playful attitude and ironic exuberance to be found in 21st-century design, which features an ongoing flirtation with organic forms and experimentation with materials and technologies. This opulently illustrated volume, with foreword and chapter introductions written by Andrej Kupetz, managing director of the German Design Council, presents pioneering work that extends our acquaintance with modern design in the most visually seductive way.

Once Upon a Chair: Design Beyond the Icon
R. Klanten, S. Ehmann, A. Kupetz and S. Moreno, editors
Gestalten
ISBN 978-3-89955-256-0

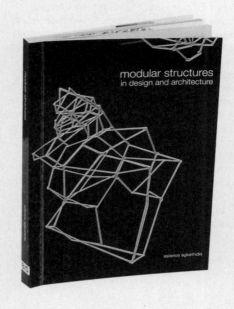

MODULAR STRUCTURES
IN DESIGN AND ARCHITECTURE

Bis Publishers introduces designers and architects to the languages of complex geometry and the cutting-edge technologies than can articulate them.

This book examines morphogenetic processes based on a combination of digital and analogue modelling and manufacturing techniques. Traditional physical modelling techniques, used together with digital 3D modelling and manufacturing technologies, result in complex constructs with additional components and/or properties. Often, these modules can be translated into architectural or industrial designs – or, as the publisher calls them, 'precursors of architecture and product design still to be realized'. Visual studies appearing in the book – produced in an academic context at the Technical University of Darmstadt, Germany – exemplify an intriguing new method of educational motivation and a systematic approach to architecture and design. They serve as an important tool with which to introduce (future) designers and architects to complex geometries and innovative CAD/CAM technologies, as well as teaching readers how to work with the new information. *Modular Structures in Design and Architecture* comes is a handy, 160-page pocket edition that features 17 projects.

Modular Structures in Design and Architecture
Asterios Agkathidis, author
Bis Publishers
ISBN 978-90-6369-206-3

NEW TECHNOLOGIES

With global networks and digital communication playing increasingly important roles in our lives, Phaidon explores their influence on product design in New Technologies.

As an increasingly important part of everyday life, communication stimulates the rapid development of digital culture, which in turn inspires and provokes product designers – in particular, the younger generation. These newcomers to the field see design not only as the creation of beautiful, functional objects from vehicles to wristwatches, but also as a tool for remaking all aspects of contemporary life. Products resulting from digital design have changed the way we communicate, the way we travel and the way we make ourselves at home in the 21st century. This book features key designs by people who have reinvented established products and, in so doing, set up new standards in style and quality. Guiding the newbies are notables such as Philippe Starck, Ron Arad, Konstantin Grcic, Marc Newson and Jonathan Ive. Full information is supplied on each product shown, including details about the design process and the manufacturers involved. Illustrations highlight both the finished product and the often ground-breaking technology that led to each creation. Readers will find 333 classics from 1966 to the present on 1100 information-packed pages that focus on the impact of new technology on product design. This book is the third in a three-volume set. The previous publications – *Mass Production* and *Pioneers* – are available in the same format as *New Technologies*.

New Technologies: Products from
Phaidon Design Classics, Volume Three
Phaidon
ISBN 978-0-7148-5667-4

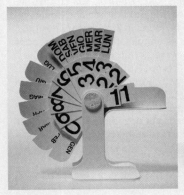

TIMOR CALENDAR (1966), ENZO MARI

TUBE CHAIR (1969), JOE COLOMBO

CHANDELIER 85 LAMPS (1993), RODY GRAUMANS

BROMPTON FOLDING BICYCLE (1975), ANDREW RITCHIE

SPAN
SPAN THE BOUNDARY BETWEEN SPACE AND GRAPHICS

Page One Publishing presents 97 projects which prove that using graphic design in interiors can result in surprising spaces.

Recent years have seen graphic design move from flat surfaces to inhabit three-dimensional shapes and spaces. Graphic design can be used to alter or distort an interior: some of the optical illusions involved visually tip a room out of balance. The effects created – often geometric in nature – result in spaces that trick the eyes. We suddenly perceive our surroundings in a different way. *SPAN* presents graphic elements and their application within various spaces, where they can evoke a certain atmosphere or generate interaction with occupants. The book offers an insight into the visual relationship between graphics and space. Projects selected include installations, stands and wall coverings. The work shown covers the use of graphic design indoors and out. Each carefully chosen project is supported by illustrations and texts that often reveal the designer's source of inspiration. Several projects have confusing photo captions, however, and the book design itself leaves much to be desired: the decision to use different kinds of paper, for example, spoils the appearance of the spreads. Then, too, certain images are synchronized poorly in terms of focus, quality and colour.

SPAN: Span the Boundary between Space and Graphics
Wang Shaoqiang, editor
Page One Publishing
ISBN 978-981-245-781-3

CAREFUL, IT'S FRAGILE!

CERAMICS AND GLASS no longer fall into simple categories like 'functional' or 'pretty'. Designers are using these materials to communicate facts and to underline traditions.

01
ONETEAKETTLE

Winner of the 2009 World Kitchen Tea Off competition, Oneteakettle was 'designed with both boiling and serving in mind'. As the filled kettle heats on the stove, graphics on its surface – applied with thermochromic ink – slowly appear until they are fully visible and the tea is ready. A magnetic trivet allows the kettle to be placed safely on a table.
Vessel Ideation
vesselideation.com

02
NEUTRAL/STEEL GREY BANDED BOTTLE
BY CALEB SIEMON

The rich hues and undulating topography of Southern California provide Caleb Siemon with inspiration for his collection of 'banded bottles'. Siemon applies alternating layers of opaque and transparent colour to clear, lead-free crystal. Where colours overlap, new ones are formed, adding depth to the various vases and vessels.
calebsiemon.com

03
TEA TIME
BY ANIEK MEELDIJK

Omitting shadows would be a shame: it's a thought that surely occurred to Aniek Meeldijk as she approached the design of her otherwise rather traditional tea set. Intangible outlines ask not only to be used, but also to be seen and experienced. This takes time. Tea time.
aniekmeeldijk.com

04
LOOKING GLASS
BY SEBASTIAN BERGNE

Surely *Alice in Wonderland* flashes to mind when you see this upside-down decanter made of borosilicate glass. Sebastian Bergne's Looking Glass features a liquid-filled magnifying lens. Place the carafe next to food, objects or table guests for an exaggerated view of reality.
sebastianbergne.com

05

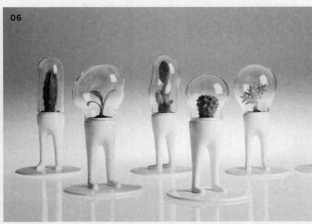
06

07

08

09

10
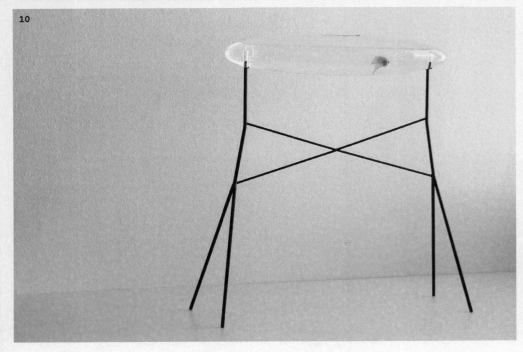

05
SKY PLANTER
BY PATRICK MORRIS

Patrick Morris's Sky Planter invites us to look up and enjoy plants from a unique perspective. No longer will pot plants be relegated to an out-of-the-way corner. A simple locking disc holds both plant and soil in place, and a revolutionary reservoir system gradually feeds water to the roots of the plant. Visit YouTube to see how it works.

Boskke
boskke.com

06
DOMSAI
BY MATTEO CIBIC

Little hand-blown bell jars on ceramic legs add a spark of personality – and a green manifesto – to the office or home environment. Handcrafted in Italy, each Domsai is unique. The dome can be lifted when the plant needs watering.

Monotono
monotono.it

07
POLAROID FLOWER VASE
BY JUNG HWA-JIN

A new take on the perennial pendant lamp, Polaroid Flower Vase reflects both a desire to cherish old memories and a nod to nature. Jung Hwa-Jin's design features a tiny pot and a Polaroid-size frame with a built-in light that illuminates the plant and encourages it to grow.

junghwajin.com

08
LP 08 // D1.2.1
BY LAURA PREGGER

By cutting and combining existing objects, altering surfaces, and manipulating the function of finished and half-finished pieces of porcelain, Laura Pregger provides everyday objects with new contexts. Her work is defined by contrasts such as 'traditional versus contemporary' and 'familiar versus strange'.

laurapregger.ch

09
CONTEM/PLATE
BY JAY BAKKER

Jay Bakker covered Wedgwood plates with images of graffiti found along Dutch motorway A2. He combined these photographs with a gold 'working mechanism' that depicts coronary vascular disease.

jaybakker.nl

10
AIR 1 AQUARIUM
BY AMAURY POUDRAY

French designer Amaury Poudray has created an elegant object that he says creates 'a link between two materials': tenuous steel legs support a sleek, elongated glass aquarium. He also compares the design to 'writing, which combines letters to create meaning'. The fish, unfortunately, declined to be interviewed.

USIN-e Designers
usin-e.fr

11

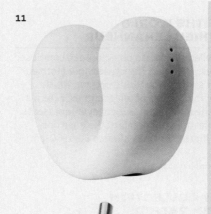

12

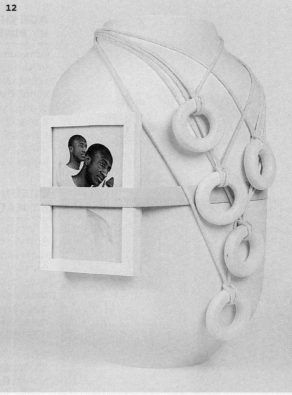

13

14

15

11
DOLLY
BY ROSS MCBRIDE

The result of an experiment, Dolly is attractive, humorous and functional. Ross McBride's sculptural, feminine salt-and-pepper pot adds a talking point to the table. Dishwater safe (remove bottom plug first). Dimensions: 10.5 x 7.5 cm.

Normann Copenhagen
normann-copenhagen.com

12
MOULDING TRADITION
BY SIMONE FARRESIN AND ANDREA TRIMARCHI

Moulding Tradition – the designers' perspective on the ephemeral concept of tradition – displays the contradictions of a decadent culture and focuses on the migration of Africans to Lampedusa Island, Sicily. These vases, which depict the faces of anonymous immigrants, explore a tradition of craftsmanship rooted in the past and still alive today.

FormaFantasma
formafantasma.com

13
THE KILLING OF THE PIGGY BANK
BY MARCEL WANDERS

This porcelain object is the latest edition to the Delft Blue Collection by Marcel Wanders and Royal Delft. It represents the digital age of currency and the fast-approaching extinction of physical money. According to Mooi, it 'illustrates the precise moment the piggy bank is struck'.

Moooi
moooi.com

14
99 FEELINGS
BY MITSY SLEURS

Belgian artisan Mitsy Sleurs created 99 Feelings: small objects that reveal an incredibly wide range of emotions. The omission of number 100 represents all the feelings Sleurs has left unexpressed. Each of her 'babushkas' features a unique texture or an addition to the basic shape.

artmind-etcetera.blogspot.com

15
OBJECT OF SOUND
BY NOCC

This candleholder is part of the Object of Sound project by Paris-based designers NOCC. The three-dimensional form of each piece in the collection is generated by the shape of sound waves as the name of the object is pronounced. Differences in shape are due to differences in individual voices as they say the same word.

Self Studio
self-studio.com

16

16
AGE OF THE WORLD
BY MATHIEU LEHANNEUR

Ten enamelled terracotta objects, each composed of 100 layers, make up French designer Mathieu Lehanneur's Age of the World project, which charts the populations of ten countries, in terms of age, in the form of urns. Each layer represents a year of life: the birth ring is at the base and the death ring at the apex of each 60-x-60-cm 'pagoda'.

mathieulehanneur.com

17

17
CREEMY COLLECTION
BY KARIM RASHID

Fine bone china in pristine white was Karim Rashid's choice for his creemy tea & coffee collection, which includes a coffee pot, a tea pot, cups and saucers for both beverages, a sugar bowl, a creamer and, for the Italian-at-heart among us, an espresso cup and saucer. Winner of a 2008 red dot design award.

Gaia&Gino
gaiagino.com

18
BOULES
BY INGRID RUEGEMER

Delicate lenses integrated into each distinctive tumbler add a playful aspect to Ingrid Ruegemer's tactile, hand-blown designs. Heavy curved bases allow the glasses to rock without tipping over. Each Boule is 11 cm high and 9.5 cm in diameter.

Absolute Appetite
absolute-appetite.com

18

19

19
THE BASTARDS HAVE LANDED
BY SIMON KLENELL

Designed and made by Simon Klenell, these gleaming, sculptural, glass objects express what the designer calls 'a functional language'. Tables pictured here were designed and produced by Klenell and colleague Kristoffer Sundin.

konstfack2009.se

20
KAARSRECHT GLAS
BY PASCAL SMELIK

A great example of 'breaking the mould'. Dutch designer Pascal Smelik has created a collection of wine glasses by plunging hot wax into cold water and making casts from the resulting forms. Smelik's aim was to give each goblet a unique shape.

Kaarsrecht
kaarsrecht.wordpress.com

20

21

21
MILKY WAY
BY ANNA EHRNER

'Experimental stylist' Anna Ehrner uses special glass-on-glass techniques for Milky Way, a collection of objects she created for Swedish firm Kosta Boda. To celebrate Milky Way's five-year anniversary, Ehrner designed special 'touch of silver' pieces for the collection.

Kosta Boda
kostaboda.com

H&M HOME IN STOCKHOLM BY UXUS
PHOTO DIM BALSEM

MERCI IN PARIS BY MARIE-FRANCE AND BERNARD COHEN
PHOTO TARA BRADFORD

NEXT ISSUE
73
Play it Again

In the next issue, *Frame* focuses on fun, visiting playful interiors like ARNE QUINZE's L'Eclaireur store in Paris, made using two tonnes of timber and 147 video screens, and SERGIO CALATRONI's joyfully tongue-in-cheek EMPORIUM SHOP in Tokyo. Then we're off to Israel, to check out whether RON ARAD's rusty arabesque extravaganza looks as good on the inside as outward appearances suggest. We catch up with COMME DES GARÇONS' latest adventures in Black and even try to answer the age-old question: why don't men like shopping?

MARZ GALLERY IN LISBON BY MIGUEL VIEIRA BAPTISTA
PHOTO FERNANDO GUERRA I FG+SG

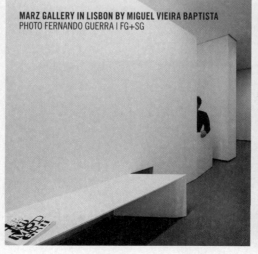

L'ECLAIREUR IN PARIS BY ARNE QUINZE
PHOTO DAVE BRUEL